# AUDLEY HARRISON
## Realising the Dream

Challenge yourself daily and live everyday as if it's the last. Tomorrow is promised to no one.

*Audley Harrison*

# AUDLEY HARRISON

## *Realising the Dream*

Audley Harrison
as told to Niall Edworthy

GRANADA

First published in Great Britain in 2001

By Granada Media, an imprint of André Deutsch
Carlton Publishing Group
20 Mortimer Street
London W1T 3JW

In association with Granada Media Group

A catalogue record for this book is available from the British Library.

ISBN 0 233 99999 X

Plate section/photographs
Allsport/Al Bello, John Gichigi, Alex Livesey, Craig Prentis;
Empics/Neal Simpson; PA Photos/Toby Melville, Fiona Hanson,
Rebecca Naden, Toby Melville, EPA; and courtesy of Audley Harrison.

Typeset by
Derek Doyle and Associates, Liverpool
Printed and bound in Great Britain

2 4 6 8 10 9 7 5 3 1

www.AudleyHarrison.com

# Contents

# Acknowledgements

I would like to extend a special thank you to all the individuals (you know who you are) who have doubted my desire to make something of my life. Your apathy towards me has been inspirational in motivating me to succeed and prove that the world really is your oyster, if you want it badly enough.

So many people have contributed to my success, touching me with their wisdom and guidance, and these people, along with the important episodes in my life, are described in this book. However, there are some people I would especially like to thank.

A special mention must go to my father who had the temperament to keep his four boys together when his marriage broke down and tried his best to bring us up. Although I didn't appreciate my Dad's parenting methodology at the time, it has made me the person I am today.

I would like to thank my brothers, especially Rodney, for their encouragement and support in keeping my feet on the ground, although I know I drive them crazy with my demanding ways. I wish them success and happiness and hope we can continue to build our brotherly love so that we can really be united. Another special mention goes to Hazel whom I regard as my true soul mate and the sister I've always wished for. Big up to Paul, my best mate, and all the boys in the hood!

So many individuals have had a positive influence on me but don't get a mention in this book, so here is my thank you to them. They are the friends and acquaintances who have bonded with me and loved me for me: Audley. To anyone else who has influenced me that I have failed to mention: my apologies.

Mr Docrat, Mr Randower, Miss Mason from Harlesden Primary School; Sue from Northwood Covenants Church Club; Doug Williams from Whitmore High School; John, Jane and Oliva from the College of North East London; Sharon Todd, Tom Tranter, Greg DeSilva, Miss Gervis, Craig Sharp and Andy Lane from Brunel University. From the world of amateur boxing: Simon Kemp, Peter Davis, Bill Shepherd, all my boxing comrades from Repton and England, plus all the committee members from my boxing club at Brunel, especially Vicki and Errol; Peter from Pinner Cricket Club. From the British Olympic Association: Steven Martin, Cathy Green, Marzena, Anne, Nick Fellows, Luke, Laura, Lyn, all the Gold Coast personnel and medical team and the Commonwealth Games and Olympic Village support staff and medical teams. Your support for me was unwavering before, during and after the respective tournaments. From the world of professional boxing, Lloyd Honeghan, Naseem Hamed, Adrian Ogun, Geraldine, Gary Mason, Chris Eubank and sparring partners Michael Sprott, Gary Delaney, Chris Woolas, Harry Senior and Joseph Young. Bev and all at the Nerrang Boxing Club. All the staff at the Hustyns Resort, especially Ivan, for their impeccable services. Also Charlie Magri Sports, Lonsdale and Mandalay Bay, Las Vegas. The staff at the North-west London Housing Association in Hounslow who gave me sound advice as a wild and unsure nineteen-year-old and Alastair at Atkins House for writing that song with me and teaching me the piano.

Also a big thank you to my co-author Niall who battled

against adversity and personal dramas to complete this book in record time. Thanks also to the staff at Granada for their patience and Lindsey for keeping them calm as my eagerness to put the final touches on the book meant rewriting a few chapters, which didn't go down too well.

My biggest gratitude is to God, for He has blessed me with an inner spirit that refuses to read the script. Through His blessing I found boxing and through boxing I found myself.

I hope you enjoy this book, especially if you are a teenager, getting into trouble and being told by your parents, teachers or institutions that you will become nothing if you don't do as you are told. Your pathway is out there and only you can find it. Begin to dream and set the goals that will allow you to over-come all obstacles and make a success of your life. Let nothing or no one stand in the way of realising your dream.

Audley Harrison
September 2001

# Introduction

Clutching the gold medal in my pocket, I was jogging down the road in the Olympic village hurrying to get changed for the closing ceremony. As I turned a corner, the full emotional force of what I had achieved hit me. The entire British team, about three hundred of them, were there ready to set off to the Olympic Stadium. When they caught sight of me coming they all broke into a spontaneous round of applause, clapping and shouting their congratulations and slapping me on the back as the crowd parted to let me through. The emotion started welling up inside me and for a moment I thought I was going to lose it.

Everyone has their moment: for some it is on the podium, for others it is straight after the event, and for yet others it might not happen for years and then it hits them out of the blue as they are sitting in their garden or walking down the street. This was my moment, where the full enormity of it punched me smack on the chin and left me needing an emotional standing count. Here were all these guys and girls I had been living with cheek-by-jowl for over a month and who had become a temporary, extended family. As they mobbed me it felt like I had come home after some great adventure like a voyage around the world. I bit my lip and kept my head down in case anyone saw that I was getting emotional, and then I ran up to my room to dump my gear and get ready for the celebrations, swallowing hard and fighting back the emotion. You can laugh if you want, but you try winning an Olympic gold medal after everyone has told you that your life is going nowhere.

About twelve years earlier my childhood had effectively come to an end when the reinforced cell door at Feltham Young Offenders' Institute was slammed shut behind me. As I sat down on my bed I heard the screw turning the key in the lock before slowly trudging off down the corridor. Over the next couple of years or so I would spend a total of eighteen months in detention, either on remand between trials or serving my sentence after conviction. I would be in my twentieth year before I could once again breathe air as a free man.

Sociologists and child psychiatrists would no doubt tell you that the early life of Audley Harrison is a textbook example of how not to grow up: broken home, a mother I never saw, a father at work all day, expelled from two schools before leaving with no qualifications, petty misdemeanours leading to more serious crime (gang warfare, train surfing, graffiti, street robbery), no job, no money, no prospects, very good at most sports but probably not good enough to make a career of any of them. To the outside world, mine might have seemed like a life without hope.

While I was in prison, I remember one of the prison officers saying, 'Dear, oh dear, whatever are we going to do with you, Audley? You should think about sorting your life out.'

Ten years later, as I write this, I am an Olympic and Commonwealth gold medallist, a Bachelor of Science (Hons), a Member of the Order of the British Empire, a qualified fitness instructor, a qualified assistant boxing coach, a household name, a champion of the rights of amateur boxers, financially stable and a donator to charity. I have been to

Buckingham Palace and joked with Queen Elizabeth II. I have met Prime Minister Tony Blair. I have followed in the footsteps of Bill Clinton, Nelson Mandela and Michael Jackson and addressed the Oxford Union and I am hailed as a role model for British youth today. When I was younger, people would cross the street to avoid me. Now they cross it to ask for my autograph.

These are not boasts, nor two-finger salutes to anyone who may have doubted me – they are simply the bare facts of my life. They are *my* achievements, but if they can serve as an inspiration to a new generation of adolescents who feel – or have been told – that their life is going nowhere, then my satisfaction will be all the greater. If, when I am an older man with my hair greying around the temples and a grandchild bouncing on my knee, I hear a young athlete on the television saying that he was inspired by Audley Harrison, then I will go to my grave a very happy man.

Even when my life appeared to others to be going nowhere, I always believed that I would make a success of myself somehow. I remember one night when I was about ten or eleven years old, I ran away and didn't come home for a couple of nights. My Dad set out in the car with my brothers Rowan, Terry and Rodney to find me. I was sitting on a wall outside a petrol station when the car drew up and they all jumped out and chased me down the road. They finally caught me, dragged me kicking and screaming back to the car, and pinned me down on the back seat. My Dad started shouting at me, 'What are you doing with your life, Audley? What are you doing? What are you going to make of your life?'

I shouted back, 'I'm gonna be famous! I'm gonna be famous!'

'Famous for what, Audley? It's time you grew up.'

'I don't know, but I promise I'll be famous. I promise.'

He didn't believe me, of course. But I honestly believed

3

what I was saying. I have always had a full bucket of self-belief. I knew I would make a splash – I just needed to find the right pool to jump into. It wasn't until I stepped into a boxing ring for the first time about eight years after that night that I found my ticket out of trouble, my passport to success.

# CHAPTER 1

# WILD AT HEART

I was approximately four years old when my parents' marriage broke down and my mother left home. Her leaving seemed normal – just something that happened in life. It would be easy to say it scarred me and to claim that I was some kind of innocent casualty of life's cruelty, but, as far as I can tell, the experience had no adverse impact on me. I have never in my life felt like a victim. I didn't cry at the time, and I don't recall any great feelings of loss or grief. Maybe I was too busy playing and fighting with my brothers to notice. We all just got on with the business of living: Dad, a plasterer, carried on plastering, and we boys went to school and horsed around at home. It's difficult to say exactly what goes through the mind of a child at that age, but for as long as I can remember my attitude has always been that the only person who was going to make me happy or not was myself.

Shortly after my mother left we exchanged our nice suburban house in a leafy street in Sudbury in Middlesex for a second-floor flat in a council block in the Stonebridge area of Harlesden, north-west London, a few miles further into town. It was – and still is – a mainly black area with a really strong community spirit. My most vivid memories of it are going to Tavistock Saturday church school and playing with the other kids in the local adventure playground. I also remember the summer camps organised by the social services when all the youngsters would go off to a castle called Tinley Hall in the countryside for a couple of weeks of games and activities. Later, in my early teens, I also went to the local church (of England) and to church classes until my early teens. Nowadays I rarely attend church and I have little interest in it as an institution, but I still talk to God. For me, faith and prayer are a personal matter, whether you are Christian, Buddhist, Sikh, Muslim, Hindu or Jew. It's about my relationship with my Maker, not about standing in a pew reading from a prayer book. I always say my prayers and I genuinely feel as if God is watching out for me. It would be wrong to say that I am a devout Christian in the strict sense of the phrase, but I am a man of faith.

We lived in Stonebridge until I was about eleven years old before Dad moved us out to another leafy suburb, Pinner, because he felt that there would be less chance of us getting into trouble on the streets there. His business was going well and he had plastered so many people's homes that he ended up being able to afford one of his own. Stonebridge is a rough, tough inner-city neighbourhood compared to Pinner and, even though we moved away, I would end up spending a lot of my teenage years on its streets. Pinner also had its trouble spots, especially around the Greenway where we lived and where I would hang around with the other kids, getting up to mischief and causing a bit of trouble.

Although we probably didn't appreciate it at the time, our father did a brilliant job bringing four boys up on his own. When my Mum left, Dad had thought about getting us all adopted but once he heard it was highly unlikely that all four of us would be taken in by the same family, he decided to bring us up himself. He couldn't stand the thought of us all being split up. It must have been tough having to go out to work every day while making sure we were fed, clothed and generally looked after. Dad tried to cook for us every now and then, though I'm sure he would be the first to admit that he is no Delia Smith. But he always made sure we had good food in our stomachs, and throughout our childhood there was a constant stream of aunties and family friends passing through our house.

My Dad is a decent, hard-working man who has tried to live his life obeying the law. He taught us all the difference between right and wrong. Dad, however, was not someone who could communicate very well with us, so from an early age I was forced to use my initiative and make my own decisions. Even when I was getting into big trouble as a teenager, I knew I was doing wrong. Most West Indian parents will give their kids a sound beating when they have done something wicked and my Dad certainly gave me a few whacks. If he had just said, 'You're a naughty boy, Audley' and done nothing else I would have thought I could get away with anything, but when Dad gave me a hiding I sure knew that I had stepped out of line. Your average West Indian family is a strong unit and the Dad is the central figure – what he says goes, and if you push it too far you get outcast.

I grew up quickly as a young boy – because I had to. If I had spent the whole of my childhood indoors watching cartoons and playing video games I would have grown up a lot more slowly. But from the age of about eight or nine I was hanging out on the streets and down at the local youth clubs. Harlesden is not Disneyland, and you only have to spend a short time on its streets to become aware that life is no Mickey Mouse cartoon. At first I would stick close with my brothers. We have always been a close band, but early in our lives we began to branch away, make our own friends and forge our own identities. As kids we quarrelled a lot but we have learned to love each other as brothers again and now we're older we are a very united group. Rowan is the oldest, but behaves like the youngest. He is the joker in the family pack, always larking around trying to get a laugh. Terry is the second oldest, one year my senior, and the quiet one of the family. He is a good footballer, a left wing back who plays semi-professional for Kingsbury. Rodney is the youngest and I probably spend more time with him than with the others. If I go out clubbing or partying, I go with Rodney. He was a decent amateur boxer, a light-middleweight, until the doctors discovered he had an abnormality on his skull that forced him to give it up.

As for my Mum, I honestly couldn't tell you what she was like because I know her only slightly better than you do. I don't see her. All I know is that she was a nurse, continues to live in north-west London and has had three more children, two girls and a boy (I believe), but I never see them either. It is a quarter of century since she left home and I have seen her only three times since then. I came across her in the mid-1990s in a supermarket. We were walking towards each other pushing our shopping trolleys, and as we got closer I realised that it was her. We looked at each other and I was about to say 'Hello' but she didn't recognise me. She was with her husband and daughter. I laughed to myself about the situation – me shopping in the same store as my mother and her being totally unaware of me. As I walked past her I said, 'God will have His way' and all three of them looked up at me. A couple of minutes later we passed each other in another aisle and I said it again, 'God will have His Way.' She looked up at me and said: 'Do I know you?' I looked at her in disbelief and said, 'I came out of your ****** and you don't know who I am?' She came closer and stared at me before saying, 'Is that you, Audley?' I turned away as she came towards me and I said,

'Move away from me or I'll embarrass you in front of all these people.' I made sure I reached the checkout till before them and once I had paid I waited by the exit until they approached with their trolley. I shouted across the store, 'Goodbye mother!' Her daughter let out an embarrassed laugh and my mother just stared as I left the shop.

The last time I saw her was early in 2000. I was sitting in a hair salon with my friend Paul waiting to be seen when my mother walked in. When she caught sight of us she came straight over and said, 'Hello how are you?' But she was addressing Paul, not me. She had met Paul a few weeks earlier in the same salon and she chatted away with him like an old friend without registering that it was her son sitting next to him. Paul obviously didn't realise what was going on either and so I tapped him on the shoulder and whispered, 'That's my Mum you're talking to.' Paul turned to my mother and said, 'You should take a close look at the person sitting on my left.' She leaned over to see who I was and I lowered my shades and peered up at her. We spoke briefly and she told all the people who work in the store that I was her son, but I don't think they believed her. Her husband came over and we all exchanged pleasantries and phone numbers before going on our separate ways. We haven't spoken since.

When I was about fourteen we had met up with her for the first time since she left. We all went round to her place to have dinner, but the evening just didn't work. It was an odd atmosphere and it felt like we were in the house of a stranger. There is no bond between us. She's just another woman. But she has stuck with the guy she married second time around, so she can't be that bad. Obviously, her relationship with my Dad was not a match made in heaven. It just happens like that sometimes. I have no strong feelings about her and I can honestly say there has never been a day when I have thought, 'Gosh, my life would be so much better if Mum hadn't left.'

Far from being unhappy, I loved growing up playing around on the estates and in the streets. As I grew into my teens I would spend less time with my brothers and more and more time with my own gang of friends. We were mischief-makers just like all young kids, with no sense of danger or fear. But as I grew older mischief turned to misdemeanour, and misdemeanour would eventually turn to crime. Although I cannot escape the fact that I am an ex-convict, I never thought of myself as a criminal. I was just someone who got into trouble and got caught. The difference between mischief and crime is fairly blurred for a young teenager. You don't deliberately set out on a path of crime, having ruled out the alternatives with the local careers officer. I just drifted into trouble with no conscious malice on my part. I never felt like a bad guy. I was a thrill-seeking, bored teenager brought up in a tough street environment and bursting with energy and aggression. Playing cat-and-mouse with the police was an amusement or a diversion, just something to do to get the adolescent adrenalin up. I was always looking for the next adventure, something to challenge me.

Getting involved in fights with other gangs was just something that happened. Where I grew up trouble just hung in the air like the clouds. The older I became the more I lived on the edge, the more risks I took: scraps turned from harmless fist fights to serious assaults involving bottles, knives and knuckledusters. It was just the world I lived in and I knew no other. But only very rarely did I purposely go looking for serious trouble. From an early age I realised that, unlike many of my contemporaries, I had the gift of the gab. I could always talk or smile my way out of a situation or defuse it with a couple of jokes. I have always been a good communicator and prefer getting on with people and winding others up to clash with one other.

Yet despite the dangerous situations I ended up in almost

daily as a teenager, I never came to any harm myself. Three of my friends were killed, some have been shot, some knifed, some have gone on the run and some are inside for life, but I somehow managed to walk through the minefield of my adolescence unscathed. I have gone on record several times to say that I think I am God-blessed, and I see the way my life has panned out as proof of that.

Almost all of my mates have seen someone die, but I haven't. I've seen people being badly beaten up and I witnessed two shooting incidents when I worked as a bouncer in the East End, but I have never seen anyone killed and I have never been around when tragedy has struck. That may not sound very strange to people who have grown up in Britain's safer neighbourhoods, but if you have spent ten or eleven years hanging around on the streets and estates of London's rougher areas and working in some of the toughest night clubs in town as a doorman, take my word for it that *not* to have seen someone die is the exception rather than the norm. I always missed the events that could have had a bad effect on me and, though it may sound silly, I honestly feel I've been protected from above, as if someone up there has guided me clear of danger.

For instance, for several years my friends and I used to go train-surfing on the Metropolitan Line. Train-surfing involves riding on top of the train and getting back inside the carriage before the train reaches a tunnel. There were groups of us who used to do it regularly, but there was one evening when I couldn't go because I was playing in a football match. When I got home I was told that a friend of ours, Scott, had died. He was drunk and had been killed instantly when he hit a bridge in the dark. That could have been me.

Another thing we used to do for thrills was climb out of the doors at the end of the carriages and hang off the side of the train and wave at people inside. One of the guys in my gang was killed when he struck a metal pylon as he swung out from between the carriages but once again I wasn't there because I had decided to stay at home that night. Spraying graffiti on buildings alongside railway lines was another favourite pastime at this age, and one of our gang was killed. While he was under the platform, his jacket got caught as a train pulled in and he was dragged along the track.

We were adrenalin-junkies with no fear of anybody or anything. We used to climb buildings and garages and jump from one to the other, and several of my friends broke their limbs in the process. But for all the crazy, dangerous things we did, the only serious accident that ever happened to me was falling from a tree in Byron Park in Sudbury and breaking my arm.

I have lost touch with most of my friends from this period but recently friends like T-Reg, Chalkie, Jason Craig, Matthew Baker and Hedgie have all made contact. They have all settled down and some have got married, but other people I grew up with have got involved in more serious trouble and some have even ended up being killed in turf wars. For a lot of my friends, and for others whom I knew less well, relatively harmless mischief turned into something much more danger-ous as they grew older. For a start, there weren't guns when we were growing up. At some time in our youth we all carried some sort of weapon and went looking for trouble in the West End – but we never, ever carried a gun. But today there are a lot of guns in circulation, and incidents which might have ended in a brawl a few years ago often now end in a shooting. You read all this rubbish about Yardie gun crime, but it's not a bunch of Jamaicans who come over for a few weeks, do a bit of shooting and fly home. It's British guys, just London kids on the streets, not some mysterious group of organised crim-inals from the Caribbean.

We used to go looking for trouble up West on a Friday and

Saturday night. Astoria, Busbys and Camden Palace were the night clubs we would head for, but if we couldn't get in, or after we had left, we would hunt out a confrontation. Some of the worst trouble used to take place on the N18 night bus, which headed west from Trafalgar Square via Paddington, the Harrow Road, Kensal Green and Harlesden up to Wembley. The N18 became a tourist bus for gangs: there were fights, people getting robbed, girls getting abused. The trouble was so bad and so constant that it became the first London night bus to have cameras installed.

I'm not proud of everything I used to get up to as a teenager, but at that time it just seemed like tomfoolery. Most of the trouble involved showdowns with other gangs, and we didn't go around randomly terrorising total strangers. It was like Cowboys and Indians for inner-city adolescents. It may sound strange, but hanging around in a gang on the streets of London taught me all about loyalty, team spirit and, to some extent, patriotism.

Club fighting in London is very territorial and there is fierce rivalry between the gyms from different parts of the city. When I boxed, first for Northolt and then for the Repton Boys' Club in Bethnal Green, I fought not just for my own pride and status but also for the reputation of the gym. The individual rivalry between boxers in the same weight category from different gyms can be even more intense, especially between the black boxers. A black boxer from Harlesden and a black boxer from Brixton, for instance, will be fighting for the honour of their community more than anything else, just as they might have been a few years earlier on the streets of the West End.

I didn't realise how patriotic I was until I got involved in international competition. Looking back, I can see I knew patriotism – though only on a much smaller, local scale. I was proud of being a Londoner, but even more proud of being one from the north-west of the capital. I had only been out of London a couple of times before my twenties and didn't go abroad until I was twenty-two when I went to Crete with Hazel (more about her later). I lived in a small world, and it wasn't until I started fighting for England in the late-1990s that I realised I belonged to a much wider community. At a major international event you've got the Cubans running around with their flags or draping them around their bodies, the Americans chanting 'U-S-A! U-S-A!', the British singing 'Rule Britannia' and so on. I recognised the surge of pride and deter- mination I felt at these events as something similar to what I had experienced when I was hanging around in a gang in London. When gangs used to come in from other areas and start taking liberties, we felt it was a matter of honour to defend our patch. There is a similar dynamic going on with patriotism – it is territorial, local pride, gang warfare on a grand scale, and I feel for Britain now what I felt for Stonebridge as a teenager. It's where I come from, and I'm proud of it.

The first time I felt a big surge of patriotism was at the 1998 Commonwealth Games, but that was multiplied a hundred times in Sydney when every country in the world was there and the British fans were absolutely brilliant. It made my spine tingle and sent goose pimples shimmering up my arms as I looked at the faces of all these strangers in the crowd who were cheering for me like I was their brother. As I stood there in the ring before the start of each of my fights it was brought home to me that it wasn't just my hopes I was trying to fulfil, but also the hopes of hundreds of thousands of other Brits. It was a weird, slightly overwhelming feeling at first, but once I got on top of it it gave me a soaring boost, like I had just drunk a bucket of adrenalin. It was both daunting and thrilling to know that as I stood there in the ring there were people all over Britain, from Inverness to Penzance, setting their alarms in the middle of the night to come downstairs to watch me fight. Like the other leading Olympians, I was carrying the responsibilities of other people's dreams; and to know that I gave people a lift and made them feel a bit better about themselves, or a little more proud of their country, was a deeply satisfying feeling.

I remember when I was very young I stayed up to watch Liverpool win the European Cup in the early 1980s and then basked in their reflected glory for days on end. It almost felt as if *I* had achieved something. A dozen or so years later, to know that people were going off to work with a spring in their step after watching me in action at the Olympics was a humbling thought. You might think it would make someone feel big-headed, but in fact it is the opposite. You feel flattered and honoured that people have invested so much hope and faith in you. I knew at the time in Sydney that a lot of people were getting behind me back in England, especially as I progressed towards the final, but I did not realise the full extent of that support till I got back. When I left for Sydney I could walk down the street without being recognised. But when I got back, everybody was going, 'Well, done Aud! . . . Nice one, mate. . . . You did us proud. . . .'

It's difficult to describe unless you have actually experienced the adoration of strangers, but when I came back from Sydney Britain felt like more of a home than it had ever done before. It was as if I had tapped into some great reservoir of other people's feelings and become part of a much wider community.

I loved my schooldays, although it is highly unlikely that most of my teachers would say they enjoyed those years as much as I did. I was every teacher's nightmare. Academically I was terrible and left without a single qualification. The only pieces of paper I had when I left secondary education were two expulsion letters. I had the concentration levels of a Yorkshire terrier. If I had ever had reason to draw up a CV, it would have read like this:

Harrison, Audley
GCSEs: none
A levels: none
Schools expelled from: two
Hobbies: train-surfing, graffiti, gang fighting, bullying, snogging girls, stealing other boys' dinner money, general mischief, various sports

But I knew I was a sharp kid. When I was really young I had these dimples and a big smile, which made it virtually impossible for my teachers to punish me (or so they told me later). I would do something really naughty in the class and when the teacher shouted, 'What the hell are you doing now, Harrison?' I would just flash them my coy Lady Di smile. I think my teachers would say they liked me, but found me a pain in the neck. The only question I asked when I was at school was 'Why?' I would challenge everything. I was not a malicious kid, although I did go through a bad, bullying stage when I was older. I was inquisitive, confident and mischievous and had no interest in studies. I was always stirring up trouble, and when teachers shouted at me it had no effect. It never panicked or cowed me. I just used to smile back at them, like we were playing some kind of game. There's not much teachers can do when they are faced by someone like me, and remembering now how I behaved, they have my full sympathy.

Some of the teachers I genuinely got on really well with. They were the ones who didn't get angry with me. They would laugh at my jokes and pranks, accepting that that was just the way I was. I respected them, and in their classes I was much better behaved. They were able to see the good in me and they didn't feel threatened by my anarchic attitude. I've always been like that with authority – if someone comes at me with attitude, they'll get it back and worse. If they're nice, I'm nice. I'm only confrontational when I'm challenged. I'm never the first to scowl, but I've always been opinionated. I'll only ever do things on my own terms, never anyone else's unless their ideas happen to match mine.

Whatever social system or institution I've ended up in, I've always rebelled against the authorities. At school, in prison, in my boxing gyms, at university, with the Amateur Boxing Association, with the England set-up: everywhere I have gone, I have been surrounded by controversy. I am non-conformist, rebellious by nature, and it's not an affectation or a pose – I've always been like that. I make no apologies, because I cause trouble not for the sake of it, but to rock the status quo and change the system for the better. I'm always going to speak up for what I see as right, for myself and for my people. I always stuck up for other kids at school who didn't have the courage to do it themselves, and years later I did exactly the same for my fellow amateur boxers when they feared the reaction of the authorities.

The classes I enjoyed the most were drama and music. It probably won't come as much of a surprise to learn that I particularly liked acting and improvisation. I used to get an adrenalin thrill from people watching me as I showed off and played to the gallery. These classes seemed more real and to have a more obvious purpose than the others. It wasn't any good the geography teacher shouting at me about cumulo-nimbus clouds and rock formations. Cumulo-nimbus clouds are not important to a fourteen-year-old boy. And why would I want to learn French? We didn't have too many patisseries on Harlesden High Street. It was only much later that I began to understand the importance of education. I started all over again from the bottom, got some basic qualifications and ended up with a degree from Brunel University. But back then all I thought about was music, girls, sport and causing mischief with my mates.

Despite all the trouble I caused in the classroom, I rarely got into serious fights with other kids. Not many people wanted to fight me because I was so big and not a particularly aggressive character – until I left Wembley High at the age of twelve and went to a school called Northwood Hills, which was predominantly white. It wasn't a really hostile school but I stood out from the crowd a bit, and with so few black faces around it felt slightly alien. My way of dealing with this new environment was to become chief bully. The alternative was to compromise and become part of them, not an Uncle Tom figure so much, but just a watered down version of myself. I wanted to keep my identity and didn't want to bow to anyone, so I had to make it clear that I was not going to be messed with. I used to bully kids for their dinner tickets and then sell them back to them.

Everyone got really fed up with my constant tormenting and one day I got jumped by about ten kids – all of them white, except the leader, a mixed-race kid called David who held me down and tried to make me promise I would never bully them again. The dinner ladies broke it up, but as I got up I managed to land a lovely clobber smack on David's nose. And I had my revenge the next week when my little gang – who were all white kids too – ambushed my assailants one by one. From the earliest age I have never been someone who chooses his friends according to their colour. Some black guys want to hang with the white guys and go to the pub or whatever, and then you get the white guys who want to hang with the black guys and listen to soul music or go to the clubs. For me, I just always hung around with the cool guys, whether they were black or white. My mates were my mates. Full stop.

My bullying got slightly out of control at Northwood Hills

and I was hauled up before the head teacher on several occasions. Eventually they had enough of me terrorising the other pupils and I was expelled at the age of thirteen and sent to Whitmore High School in West Harrow. I was at Whitmore until I was fifteen, but my behavioural problems continued and I was finally transferred to a special school for troubled children, Atkins House. When I was younger I sometimes used to get roughed up myself by some of the older kids. When I was aged about ten, the older kids used to bash us about up at the adventure playground in Stonebridge if we gave them mouth. In recent years I have seen these guys around and I can't believe they used to push me around. They are so little.

Bullying, though, was just a side interest. My main hobby at school was trying to snog girls. The first girl I kissed was called Sherma, at Harlesden Primary School in Acton Lane. We used to play this game called 'riggy-riggy' when all the girls would line up at one end of the playground and all the boys at the other. Once everyone was in line the boys would shout, 'We want riggy-riggy' and then you'd run across the playground, grab the girl you wanted and tie your jumper around her and she'd have to stay with you for the rest of break. I always used to run straight for Sherma and as I was faster and bigger than most of my classmates I always used to get to her first. After a while we became an 'item' (in so far as you can when you are still reading the *Beano*) and we were always snogging behind the bike sheds.

The first girl I really wanted to go out with was called Anne-Marie, a really pretty black girl with green eyes who was at Wembley High School with me. She was the one reason why I didn't want to get transferred from there when the teachers started getting fed up with my constant troublemaking. I thought she was beautiful, and after months of effort I had just got her livened up and interested in me when I had to change schools as my Dad moved us to Pinner. It really upset me because I liked her a lot. I never got off with her, let alone went out with her, and I remember being gutted when I left and I knew my chances of seeing her had gone.

My first sexual encounter happened at my next school, Northwood Hills, and was the kind of episode that could put you off for life. I must have been about thirteen at the time and I can't remember the name of the girl. One day we went into the woods together and lay down and I was on top of her doing my thing but I wasn't remotely aroused because I didn't have the faintest clue what I was meant to be doing. On TV and in the movies men and women rolled around together and grunted, but I didn't really understand the mechanics of what was going on. Anyway, there we were like a pair of comedy wrestlers when these five girls from the nearby estate walked in on us and started taunting me and so I quickly picked myself up and ran away. This girl, it turned out, was a bit of a problem child and she – along with the girls who had come across us – went round telling everyone she was pregnant by me. A few days later I was called before the headmaster. It had become a real scandal and I was suspended. In my innocence I did not know how to defend myself, and I was too embarrassed to say that I had not even got close to penetration. A few weeks later it was discovered that the whole thing had been a hoax, but by the time every-one found out it was too late and I was regarded as a really bad boy.

I must have been about fourteen when I got my first girl-friend, Sacha, a very pretty girl who came from somewhere posh like Harefield. She and her friends came down to this disco and they were all friends of my brother Terry, and about a year or more older than me. That night we danced and had a quick snog as we were leaving and afterwards we started seeing each other regularly, but I was too shy to try anything on with her. I made out to all my mates that we were unstoppable and all she wanted to do was go to bed. Unfortunately, the truth was that I was too shy and she got fed up and ended the affair before it even really started. Back then I can honestly say I was all mouth, no trousers.

I used to tell everyone I was twelve when I lost my virginity, but it didn't actually happen till I was nearly sixteen. One night I met this girl called Mandy on the train going up to a disco in Watford with my mates. By this age, I had become really cocky. I was Mr Mouth and I thought I could charm the birds out of the trees, so I went and sat down next to her and gave her all my spiel. She liked me enough to give me her number, and a few days later I called her and we met up at her sister's house. Everyone else left and after about an hour we were on the floor of her sister's bedroom doing the deed – and this time it was for real. The whole episode must have lasted all of two minutes, and although I had pretended I was something of a veteran in the art of lovemaking I still didn't know what the hell I was doing. As far as I understood it at that stage in my life, the important thing was to make lots of animal noises and so I groaned and roared and shouted like Tarzan swinging through the jungle. I must have sounded like I was having a hernia operation with no general anaesthetic.

A few days later I was out walking around with my mates, feeling pretty pleased with myself and my general lovemaking skills, when we bumped into Mandy's mates. At the time I was hanging out with a gang in Harrow, a lot of whom came from Harlesden and the north-west London area in general. We all thought we were a bit tough and cool, but as we approached the girls, they all started cracking up and making animal noises at me. 'Hey, look, it's the animal. It's Mr Noise,' they sniggered. I wanted the ground to open up and swallow me. Mandy had told everyone about my impressive vocal performance on her sister's floor. If it had been announced on the nine o'clock news fewer people would have known about it, and for a few weeks wherever I went everyone would call me Mr Noise.

That's how I lost my virginity, but after that there was no stopping me. I jumped on the love train and got off at virtually every stop in London. I once got into trouble when I was about nineteen, shortly after getting out of prison, when I had two girlfriends at the same time. Both of them, Alison and Diane, were really pretty girls. I couldn't decide between them so I tried to enjoy the best of both worlds. Alison, though, began to suspect something was up when she found Diane's telephone number on a piece of paper. She got a friend to call the number and discovered the truth. Needless to say, neither of them were too impressed and they both got rid of me at the same time. I've been single most of my life – the longest relationship I've had was with Hazel. We went out with each other for about five years and over time we became like brother and sister while the physical side of our relationship cooled off. She became the sister I never had – and you don't sleep with your sister. So even though we grew closer as people, we began to go our separate ways romantically. We never broke up as such. The nature of our relationship just changed with time. We are still as close as ever and a lot of people don't understand our relationship, but for us it's simple: we are just the best of friends. One day I'll settle down and have kids, but I'm not rushing – whether it's to do with coming from a broken home I don't know, but I'm adamant that I will only have kids with one woman. I'm not going to mess about and split up kids from their parents. It has been difficult to have a full-time relationship in the last five years because my career has been so all-consuming and intensive. It's the price you pay for dedication to a single cause. I've had a number of girlfriends since, each lasting a few months, but none of them have been really serious. Although I play, I'm careful not to make any mistakes that could affect my future.

When I left school at the age of sixteen, I had no real idea what I wanted to do with my life. My only real passion was sport, and I played all forms of it obsessively from an early age: football, cricket, rugby, athletics, snooker, table tennis – virtually anything. If there was a club nearby, I joined it. Strangely, the only major sport I showed absolutely no interest in while I was growing up was boxing. It seems incredible now, but for my entire childhood I had as much interest in boxing as I did in origami. My indifference was all the stranger as I was obsessed by the *Rocky* films, which I used to watch over and over again round at my mate Dave Watkins' house. I must have seen each of them about twenty times, but I had no interest in watching real boxing and the idea of joining a gym never even crossed my mind until I went to watch Rodney box when I was nineteen. Rocky was my main childhood hero, followed by Ian Botham, Michael Jackson (in his Billie Jean phase) and the entire Liverpool team of the early 1980s. Sly Stallone was my only genuine connection with the boxing world, and looking back on that time I was obviously fascinated with boxing without realising it. As I watched those videos, transfixed, it never crossed my mind for a minute that I would one day be lacing up my own gloves and stepping into the ring, let alone one day standing on the podium while someone hung a gold medal around my neck.

I think the reason why I didn't get into boxing at an earlier age was because I didn't live in the right catchment area – it's just a matter of what's on your doorstep. When I was at Northwood Hills I played rugby and football because that's what the school offered; a close friend, Jason Steele, was a member of a local athletics club, so I joined that; there was a local youth club where you could play table tennis and snooker, so I joined that; there was Pinner cricket club down the road, so I joined that. But there was no boxing club within my immediate vicinity – if there was, I probably would have joined it too.

My own experience highlights the importance for governments and local authorities to provide facilities for young people. A lot of these clubs have shut down for lack of money, even though the National Lottery is starting to arrest the decline. As a direct consequence, today there are even more kids on the street doing nothing but causing mischief or sitting at home staring at a computer game and getting fat. If you live in an inner-city neighbourhood the choice is simple: sport or mischief, maybe a bit of both. But from my own experience I can say with full confidence that, had there been no sports facilities or clubs at all, there would have been one seriously scary load of mischief going down in the area. Once we were tired of train surfing and graffiti we might take the wheels off the car of the horrible bloke at the end of the road. If he was very lucky, we might even smash his windows in for him. God knows what havoc we might have caused if we hadn't also been members of all those sports and youth clubs which used to occupy so much of our time.

I was good, even very good, at most sports, although probably not quite good enough to make a career out of one of them. In athletics, sprinting, triple jump and javelin were my disciplines, while in cricket I was an all-rounder, a quick bowler and a half-decent bat and virtually impossible to get out. I played cricket for Pinner Colts and even played against the future Middlesex and England player Mark Ramprakash. I got to know Mark fairly well as a teenager because he was also a pretty useful footballer and we both used to play for Parkfield football club, although he was a couple of years older than me. Soccer was my main sport and I played with some very good players who went on to make it in the professional ranks. One of them was Rod Thomas, now at Brighton, who played for England schoolboys, and Barry Ashby, who is probably the most successful of the lot and has been doing well at Gillingham.

The standard at Parkfield was very high and several of us had trials at Watford, the biggest local team. I don't know exactly how far I could have gone in football, but with a good coach I think I could have made it as a semi-professional. My strength was my speed down the wing – I was really skinny in those days – and I could put over a good cross, but I didn't have the greatest feet – maybe because I was so tall. They say the best players are those with a low level of gravity, like Pele, Maradona, Stanley Matthews or Tom Finney. How many great footballers measuring six foot five and a half can you name? Ian Ormondroyd?

I was never the star of the team although I always craved the starring role and used to dream of scoring hat-tricks or the winning goal. Parkfield was a very strong Sunday team, one of the best in north-west London, and won lots of cups, but the teams I played for at under-fifteen and under-seventeen were the weakest in the club. We would occasionally have scouts from the professional clubs at our matches – although, strangely, whenever I looked at the touchline they never seemed to be looking at me. There was a great team spirit, a sense of brotherhood, and I used to love our training sessions at Hatch End School on Tuesday and Thursday evenings before the matches at the weekend. You'd think they would be quite rough, but they were more technical than physical challenges.

My football career came to a bone-shuddering halt when I was playing for Parkfield against a team from Chalk Hill in Brent. Both sides were very strong and lots of my mates were playing in the Chalk Hill side. I remember the moment vividly and it still makes me wince. I must have taken out about three players on the left wing when I saw this guy out of the corner of my eye hurtling towards me. He launched himself at me, Vinnie Jones-style, two-footed and studs up, straight into my ankle. I can still hear the sound of the crunch and feel the stab of acute pain. I knew I was seriously knackered from the moment it happened. My ankle was dripping blood through the sock. I was taken to hospital to get stitched up and today I still carry a big scar from the injury. I remember the nurse – resting my head in her ample bosom somehow helped ease the pain. I spent a year hobbling around on the sidelines, and when I came back I soon realised that any future I might have had in soccer was over. I had lost my speed and some of my dexterity.

With hindsight, that terrible tackle was a very important moment in my life. My footie career was over by the age of sixteen and, although I didn't make the connection at the time, it was around then that I started drifting in and out of more serious trouble. I had been channelling all my aggression and exuberance into football, and when that outlet was no longer there for me I unconsciously started looking for other ways to get rid of all that natural energy. Contact sport is great for releasing the tensions and exuberance that well up in a man, especially a red-blooded teenager with a natural aptitude for the outdoor life. I hope that one day, when I have more time, I can set up some kind of foundation that helps get kids off the streets and into the more controlled environment of sport, where you learn that there is a place for aggression and competition within set rules.

But even more importantly, if that tackle had never happened I might never have discovered boxing. I probably would have carried on plugging away at the football, and who knows where my career would have gone? I could have ended up as a semi-pro in a north-west London league while doing a bit of plastering with my Dad in between.

After school I wanted to go to Cassio's college in Watford, which specialises in sport, but I couldn't get a place because I didn't have the grades. I didn't have any really clear idea about what I wanted to do with my life, but at the back of my mind I was optimistic I could still have some kind of a career in sport. I had no coherent game plan, just a huge unfocused enthusiasm. My first proper job was stacking shelves in the local Safeways, but that only lasted a few weeks. For some reason, the daily prospect of arranging different varieties of baked beans in an aisle just didn't appeal. I worked for Dad's plastering business and on a few building projects, and during that time I started bulking up physically. I was at that age when kids start filling out anyway, but carrying around heavy loads of bricks, cement and machinery saw me quickly pile on the muscle. All four of us brothers have worked for Dad at some point – a nice safety net, knowing there is always a bit of cash available if you need it. But like most adolescents, I was pretty work-shy and a steady day job on a building site just wasn't right for me at the time.

I was sixteen years old and becoming a real handful for my Dad, constantly getting into trouble on the streets. Dad soon had enough of it and threw me out, telling me to clean up my act. He couldn't handle my brothers and me any more: we were too wild. He thought if we were old enough to get into serious trouble then we were old enough to look after ourselves. By now he had remarried – I would end up with three half-brothers, Vincent, Adam and Ben – and he wanted to have some peace at home. I don't blame him after bringing us up by himself for over twelve years.

My home was now the streets of north-west London. At night I would doss down on floors and sofas at my mates' houses and flats. Unable to play serious sport because of my injury and with no academic qualifications to help me get a decent job, I embarked on a brief career as a professional troublemaker. By the time I was seventeen, my accommodation was being provided courtesy of Her Majesty's Government.

I love London, and Britain as a whole, but north-west London will always be my turf. It's the only place I feel truly at home. I know all the streets, the shops and hundreds of people of all backgrounds. I could never live in east or south London – they might as well be foreign countries to me. If there was a flag for north-west London I would wave it. Everyone there is real to me: they are faces I have grown up with. When I travel anywhere in Britain, everyone now says, 'Hello, Aud', but that's the way it's always been for me in north-west London and the West End. All the West Indian shops and clubs in Harlesden know me: One Stop, Scandals, DJs, KD's, Tanya's. Although I am now a celebrity, everyone takes the piss out of me just like they always have, and there is none of that awkward kind of respect when people can't be natural to you because they freeze in the bright headlights of your fame. To them, I'm just Audley – Vincent's kid or Rodney's brother or whatever. I love going back there even more now, because it feels like the real world.

After the Olympics I found myself catapulted into a weird, parallel world of TV interviews, modelling sessions, film premieres, celebrity parties and charity launches. I enjoy all that in moderation, and it will always be an important part of my career so long as it doesn't interfere with the main business of my training. I am a boxer first and a celebrity second. Although I understand the importance of marketing myself, of selling Audley the brand, if I don't make it as a boxer the whole lot will go down the pan. But after a mad day on the media and celebrity merry-go-round I yearn for normal life and, if I can, I will head straight for Harlesden where I'll meet with some old mates and go to a bar or one of the West Indian restaurants for my favourite meal of jerk chicken. I find it very liberating and stabilising when I am up there because I can talk about everything except Audley Harrison – the cricket, the footie, the new shop in the high street. My old stomping ground keeps my feet firmly on the ground and provides a welcome bolthole from the hectic and bizarre world I have found myself in since standing on that top podium in the Conference Hall on the Sydney waterfront.

# CHAPTER 2
# CHILLING IN THE CHILLER

It seemed like any other day of my life at this time when I headed up to Hendon College that morning in December 1988, but within a few hours my life would be changed for ever. A while later I was arrested in connection with what had happened in the college common room, but as I sat in the police cell that night I didn't imagine even in my wildest nightmares that I would be handed a fairly stiff prison sentence. I ended up serving a total of eighteen months, twelve on remand followed by six after conviction before finally being released. It was the beginning of the end for me as a wild child, and marked the start of my life as a highly focused, responsible individual who wanted to make something of himself. Phase one of my life was drawing to a close.

I don't want to make any moral judgement about what we were doing in those days and it's easy to be smart from hindsight, but at the time it just seemed like a bit of horseplay – something that most kids of our age did. We were bad boys and we wanted people to be scared of us, to show some fear and respect. Boys are like that at that age. You develop a bullying instinct at a time when you are trying to make a mark in the world, to prove that you are a man to be reckoned with. It was bully or be bullied, and it was inevitable we would end up having brushes with the law. If you're wandering the streets of Harlesden with a bunch of other teenage lads high on testosterone and whatever else, you're not exactly going to end up heading towards the nearest antiques fair or take a hamper for a picnic in the local park. Trouble was what we were after, and there was always plenty of it there for the taking.

If you're expecting a story involving guns and knives and broken bottles I'm afraid you're going to be disappointed. It was straightforward fisticuffs. There were six of us and about the same of them. We started arguing about something and then we beat them up and robbed them of a jacket and all their money – about twenty quid in total. No one really got hurt. We pushed them around a bit, but it was the threat of violence on top of the robbery that made the sentence so severe and I wondered whether the police had tipped off the judge about my general troublemaking. I doubt if our victims even had a bruise to show for their ordeal. Taking everything into consideration, it was probably a fair punishment. If that fight had been a one-off I would have screamed injustice, but the truth is I had done a lot worse. I had been involved in much worse assaults, I had got much more money in street robberies, I had carried an offensive weapon and I had burgled. As far as I am concerned now, society deserved a good long break from me at that time and I got my just deserts in the end even though the episode itself was kids' stuff and my role was a back-seat one. (I was basically just egging the others on. I wasn't that bothered.) I was stunned when the sentence was announced, because it had seemed like nothing at the time – just a bit of pushing and shoving.

We weren't arrested at the scene and soon forgot about the scrap at the college. But a few weeks later I was taken in by the police when they made a swoop on suspects in connection with an investigation into 'steaming', the street crime where a bunch of kids rush a train and rob the passengers carriage by carriage. Because so many people are involved, convictions are pretty rare as the victim is usually unable to make a reliable ID of the perpetrators. There were about thirty of us hanging out in Harrow when they swooped on us – loads of plain clothes policemen first, and then the uniformed lads burst around the corner in their vans. We were all taken to the local police station for interrogation.

The police had no evidence that I had been involved in 'steaming', which had nothing to do with me. But my leather jacket was the same one I had been wearing in the incident at Hendon College. It was a very distinctive one, and that was all the evidence they needed to arrest and charge me. I was put on remand and held at Feltham Young Offenders' Institute awaiting trial. In fact the jacket was the *only* evidence the police had to link me with the Hendon incident, but I suppose with my size I stand out from the crowd and so it is easy for people to remember me. But my co-defendant in the case had been picked up pretty well straightaway and had kind of implicated me anyway, and the police just needed the thinnest bit of evidence to nab me.

The case went to a retrial, which was annoying, because the first trial went OK. The prosecution case was blown to bits by our defence team, and when the jury went into deliberation it was safe as houses we would be walking. The police had nothing on us and the prosecutors had been made to look very foolish. The verdict was due to be announced on the Monday, but that morning the judge phoned in sick and there had to a retrial. I was put back on remand for six months until I was given bail and sent to a hostel in Ipswich. They wanted me out of London, and it was better than being inside, but my troubles continued there. I had only been on bail for about two weeks when I got arrested for attempted robbery, which was a nightmare. I was accused of robbing a guy of his gold ring, but on this occasion it was completely untrue. I was put on remand again and sent to Norwich prison. So I was now being held on remand awaiting two trials.

Norwich prison was an experience – to say the least. I was one of about three black guys in the entire prison and I had the same sense of being the odd one out in there as I did when I first went to the predominantly white Northwood Hills School. My response was exactly the same as then – I became chief bully. I was on the youth side of the prison, where I quickly got a gang together and began to control the place. But after a month this big, hairy biker character was admitted to the prison and all the inmates I had been bullying looked to him for protection against me. I came across him for the first time in the queue in the canteen. I felt this finger poking me in the back of the head. The biker was obviously trying to tell me who was going to be the boss. Words were exchanged and a fight erupted. The screws broke it up as quickly as possible and we were taken back to our cells.

As I sat on my bed I knew I had to take decisive action or I was going to be in trouble. If I lost control of the situation and allowed this guy to take over, I would be vulnerable to people taking liberties with me. The following morning I took a sock and filled it with a couple of heavy batteries and during the fifteen-minute association period in the morning when inmates are allowed to socialise I ran downstairs and rushed the biker with my little slinger. I hit him about six times with my weapon, which left him needing about five stitches. I had defended my honour and being sent to solitary was a price worth paying for it. When it came for me to return to my normal cell, the governor told me that he was going to keep me on a separate floor away from all the other inmates, not as a punishment but for my own protection against possible revenge attacks. I stayed there for two months before my trial came up.

The trial didn't take long. The basic facts of the case were that I taunted and humiliated a so-called local hard man who I had seen around on the streets with his gang during the two and a half weeks I spent in Ipswich before my arrest. The guy was upset that I made him look like a fool and so he went to the police and told them I had robbed him of his gold ring. In court, the case was simply a matter of his word against mine. He came across very badly under cross-examination and sounded very cocky and full of himself. I played it straight and respectful and was subsequently acquitted.

But as I walked out of court I was immediately rearrested by the London police for breaking my bail conditions. How they expected me to fulfil the conditions while I was in Norwich prison I just don't know. I mean, honestly. (Just kidding, officer.) I was driven back to Feltham.

At the retrial in Acton, I just wanted to put the whole episode behind me. I was expecting a fairly lenient sentence, if convicted, having spent so long on remand. This time my co-D landed me right in it. He hadn't intended to, but the prosecution lawyers were much sharper this time round and opened him up. As the cross-examination continued, the case began to run away from us and I knew we were going to lose. Before the judge passed sentence I sat there in the dock thinking, 'There is no way I can go down for this. Of all the things I've done, it would be crazy if I got slammed up for this.' I couldn't believe it when I was sent back to prison. For once in my life I was speechless.

Feltham was nothing like as bad as I had imagined, and I have some good memories from my time in there. I wouldn't want to go back, but I learned a lot about myself while I was inside and managed to turn the whole experience into something positive. I was lucky because there were three guys in there who were well known in north-west London and were friends of my oldest brother, Rowan, and they looked after me from the moment I arrived.

Within half an hour of the cell door being locked behind me they sent me down some cigarettes, biscuits and sugar for my tea, as well as a few other luxuries. They dangled the goods out the window from where they were on the top floor and, by means of mirrors and lines of bed linen, it all got passed down to my cell. It was a welcome gesture and made me feel very secure right from the start. I never had any trouble – quite apart from these guys' protection, I quickly learned the rules of how to get on. I was also a big bloke who seemed like he could look after himself, even though I was still pretty skinny. I was with the 'in' crowd pretty well straightaway, and never had to prove myself to anyone, unlike most new inmates. I feel sorry for the guys who arrive in those places and don't have people to watch out for them. It can be pretty scary, and if you don't know how to play the game or get on with people, things can turn ugly.

The boredom caused by the monotony of the daily regime is the biggest problem when you are inside. You are woken up at about eight when one of the warders comes and bangs on the cell door. Breakfast at nine consists of porridge, tea, bread and baked beans, and is followed by 'association', when you go to the gym or hang out with the other prisoners playing pool or cards or table tennis. Then you return to your cell for a couple of hours and read a book, listen to music or have a smoke. After lunch, friends and family can visit and there is more association or team sports like football or basketball, then supper, then more association on the landing when you would watch a movie or television before you were locked up at about 10.30 pm.

Very early on in Feltham, it crossed my mind that I could build a career as a criminal. Prisons are universities for criminals. You learn so much in there that, by the time you leave, they might as well hold a graduation ceremony at which they hand you a certificate and say, 'Congratulations, Mr Harrison, you have achieved a 2:1 in criminal studies. Good luck in your career.' You hear what other people have done, and about the kind of enterprises you could get involved in when you are back on the outside, and of course you develop a brilliant list of criminal contacts should you ever want to use them. The life of a successful proper criminal – i.e. one who doesn't get caught – sounded like an easy one. A job here and a job there, and you earn yourself a few thousand quid and don't have to work the rest of the time. I thought about it for a while at a time when I was still excited by the life of a bad boy, but after a few months my perspective started to change. I wanted to make the most of myself and be proud of what I had achieved, so I decided that a life dodging the police or living in prison was not the right way forward. Crime may pay in the short term, but in the long run you're going to come a cropper. I'm not proud of my misdemeanours as a youngster, but nor am I racked with shame and guilt. It was just life as I knew it.

It may sound daft but I don't look back on my time in Feltham – or later at the Mount, a prison in Hemel Hempstead – as a bad or depressing time, or even as a waste of part of my life. At first, I thought the prison experience could only add to my aura on the street. But that changed, and as time went on I used the experience to my advantage in a different way – to improve my mind and my body. I started working out in the gym intensively whenever I had the opportunity, and even when we were sent back to our cells I carried on doing press-ups, sit-ups and pull-ups. I had always been pretty fit but I now began to develop a powerful physique and, although again I had no idea of its significance, I guess this prison experience was another important milestone on my road to becoming a successful boxer – and a student, because I also spent a lot of time reading books. When you are banged up in a cell for fourteen or fifteen hours a day, there is not a lot of choice on the entertainment front – listening to a tape or staring at the wall getting miserable. So I began to use the time constructively by improving my knowledge. It is strange to think that at school it was the fear of boredom that drove me away from books, while in prison it was the other way around – boredom drove me to read. I read whatever I found lying around: it became a form of escapism and allowed me to dream. As I lay on my bed I could forget I was in Feltham in a small cell no more than ten feet by five, and I was able to visualise myself enjoying a different type of life. The more I read, the more I became aware of my academic shortcomings, and it was while I was inside that I decided I would acquire some qualifications when I got out. I had left school without even a GCSE in woodwork, and now I wanted some to make something of my life. Although it would be a couple of years yet before the transformation would be completed, I began to realise early on during my time in Feltham that my days as a bad boy were numbered. I would be a late-comer to education, just as I would be a late-comer to boxing.

In a way, Feltham was the first real stage in my education. I learned the importance of discipline – not necessarily the kind handed out by the system itself, but the self-discipline needed to improve body, soul and mind. I also learned to be crafty, how to negotiate and get on with people, when to keep quiet and when to assert myself. I became very good at 'playing the game', and in an institution like Feltham it is a game of survival – not so much a matter of life or death (although it can be for some) but how to survive a potentially difficult and depressing experience. The trick is to try and turn a negative into a positive, to get the most out of the place, your fellow inmates and the screws without stepping out of line. The challenge is to see how much you can get away with to improve your life in there. It is a game of delicate diplomacy – if you are too confrontational with the screws, you will end up in the 'block' (solitary confinement) the whole time and you will almost certainly not be released early. It is also a game of business: trading biscuits, cigarettes and other 'exotic goods'. Everyone has their own little business running, and if you end up being sent to the block for a week someone will take over your business while you're away. As in all games, there are winners and losers. It's only harsh inside if you don't know how to play the game or aren't very good at it.

My time inside provided me with plenty of time to reflect on my life. If you are out on the street there are a lot of distractions and diversions which stop you inquiring too deeply about what direction your life might be heading. But inside you feel as if someone has pressed the 'pause' button and your life has been freeze-framed. While I was there I was thinking, 'OK, this is fine, I can handle it and I'll get something positive out of it, but I don't want to come back and do the same thing all over again.' I read that someone had said you should try everything in life once except incest and country dancing. I had tried prison, and now it was time to move on to something different.

I was generally well-behaved inside, but there was one time early on which landed me in solitary confinement. There was a bit of trouble during association and I was restrained by eight of the officers who carried me away to the 'block'. That was the only time I was frightened. Most of the screws in there were pretty decent blokes just doing a job, and some were genuinely good guys who I would happily see on the outside, but there are one or two who definitely wouldn't make it on to my Christmas card list. And when I was being dragged off to solitary confinement I thought I was going to get a terrible beating. There were quite a few deaths in custody in British prisons at the time, and I knew a lot of people who had felt the long boot of the law when being detained. But when they finally got me to the 'block' they literally just threw me in and banged the door. Solitary confinement is not an experience I would recommend. Imagine being locked in a toilet in a strange building and you will have some idea of the frustration. It's just you, four walls, a floor, a ceiling, a chair and a small uncomfortable bed. You've got no books, no extras – just three meals a day and all the wall to stare at you could ever want.

Solitary was the worst aspect of life in Feltham, and those who kept getting sent down there were eventually broken by it. That's why a lot of people come out of prison mentally unstable. You don't see the effect it has had on them until you meet them on the outside. The broken ones are generally those who were the worst when they were kids. They were still bad inside, where they tried to fight the system and so ended up in the block for much of their time. In the end they crack, and on their release they are really volatile and often twice as danger- ous as they were when they went down. The prison system wins, but the social system it is there to serve loses. The system can send people over the edge to a mental place where they don't care about anything any more.

I was eventually transferred from Feltham to the Mount where I spent six months before receiving parole and being released. There was not much difference between the two, to be honest: the same daily routine and the same rules govern- ing the game of survival inside. It was tougher than Feltham because everyone had been convicted and most people in there were pretty hardened criminals. In Feltham, there were a lot of people on remand who were released after charges were dropped or who were innocent. There, they were a bit more lenient because a lot of people were yet to be convicted – there was more an element of innocent until proven guilty. In the Mount, you had been found guilty and you were seen to be serving your proper debt to society. An example of the contrast between the two regimes was that in Feltham you could have a visitor every day, whereas once you were sentenced and sent to the Mount you were only allowed one visitor a week. My brothers often came to visit me, as well as some girlfriends, but my Dad never visited. He just wanted me to stew and he wasn't going to give me any sympathy.

Something that helped pass the time in the Mount was sport, and football in particular. I got on really well with the sports screws in there. They were different from the rest because they treated us as equals and had a laugh with us, and we respected them for that. I played for the Mount prison officers' football team, which was great because you felt you were doing normal things just as you would if you were on the outside. The team was always half officers, half inmates, and when you were asked to play you showed them respect. They gave you something, so you give them some-thing back. My six months in the Mount flew past, partly because I was playing so much sport but also because I could see the light at the end of the tunnel. It was by no means a bad experience in there and, just as I had done in Feltham, I improved my life and can honestly say that I think I grew into a man while I was there. I paid attention in the education classes, I read books, I learned about the importance of mutual respect and the subtle politics of human behaviour. When you are living together with people for such a long period of time, you learn a lot about human nature. Also, by the time I left I was as physically fit and strong as I had ever been. On the day of my release, when the great big door slammed behind me, I felt great about myself. One of the phrases I kept saying to myself the whole time I was inside was, 'Learn to love adversity and you will learn to love life.' That's what I had done inside. I was still only nineteen and it seemed that a whole world of opportunities lay ahead of me.

I had this idea that there would be a big welcoming party waiting for me outside, maybe a beautiful girl in a convertible sports car just as there was for Michael Caine at the beginning of *The Italian Job*. But there was no one there at all to pick me up because all my brothers were working. It rammed home the point that life was just going on without me. So I hopped on a bus and then a train and went to see my brother Rodney in his bedsit in Northolt. For the first two months I lived in a bail hostel in Shoot Up Hill in Kilburn, because I was at the bottom of the Housing Association list for a property of my own. I was then transferred to another bail hostel in Hounslow, out by Heathrow airport, and although I was far away from where I wanted to be in north-west London I linked up with my mates again.

It took a bit of time to adjust on the outside and, although I was determined to start afresh, get some qualifications and make something of myself, my brushes with the law were not completely over. My experience inside had set me on a better path, but my patterns of behaviour could not change overnight once I was back on the street. It takes time to be weaned off the lifestyle you were accustomed to, and it takes strength of character to redirect your life without changing your personality or compromising your old friendships. I was grateful that I had not done anything too bad and ended up in prison for much longer. I knew guys who, in all honesty, were no worse than me, but they had stabbed some-one in a fight and the guy had died and they had ended up doing life for murder. I could easily have been one of those guys. I had been in plenty of nasty fights, and it was just luck that no one had come at me when I had my knife – I cannot say what I would have done in order to protect myself or my mates in the heat of the moment. But at least I understood this after my release. In one respect I reverted to type, just hanging out on the streets with the boys, but I was now acutely aware of the potential consequences of my actions and tried to steer clear of situations that could lead to big trouble.

About five months after my release, early in 1991, I was on the top deck of a bus heading from the West End to Shepherds Bush when I got into an argument with this bloke sitting behind me. It was a freezing day and all the windows were closed. This guy was smoking and everyone wanted him to stop so I told him to put out his cigarette. He refused and I tried to reason with him, but he blew smoke, first, on the back of my head and then into the side of my face. By this stage I was boiling and I couldn't just sit there and let him show me such disrespect, so the row escalated into fisticuffs. It was a straightforward fight, which I won, so when the police came it looked like I was the aggressor.

I was put back on remand before my trial and I was really upset to be back inside. It's the last place I wanted to be, and I also felt aggrieved that I had ended up in trouble when I hadn't gone looking for it. The other guy had provoked it. I had simply told him to put his cigarette out, but when he got aggressive I wasn't going to back down. If he was prepared to fight me about it, then good luck to him. I didn't imagine at the time that I would end up inside again. I was accused of stabbing the guy, but this was completely untrue. During the fight a handrail broke off, and he fell on to it when he went over the seat.

It was early summer and all the girls were out looking pretty, and while all my mates were chilling I was back in the chiller. As I sat in my cell I vowed to myself that from now on I would be on the straight and narrow. I was dying to get on with my life and I had had enough of time in the cells, interviews down the police station, meetings with solicitors, hanging around inside courts, listening to barristers and judges burbling away. It was like my life was in the hands of other people. I was just a number in the system being shunted from one cell to the next, from one court to another.

I agreed to a charge of ABH, and the doctor who gave evidence at the trial said there was nothing to suggest that the guy had been stabbed. I was fined £100, a token punishment. The judge seemed to recognise that I hadn't attacked the guy: a fight had developed and I had won.

After my release from Feltham I continued to live in Hounslow, and when I wasn't working for my Dad, labouring or plastering, I was on the dole. It was around this time that I met Hazel, who would become my girlfriend and one of the most important influences in my life. We met in a south London club called King on the Rye in Peckham. She was a twenty-six-year-old accountant and I was a twenty-year-old ex-con. I told her I was twenty-four so she might be more interested in me. We just clicked as a pair from the beginning, and I started to spend less time with the boys and more with her. She had never been in trouble in her life, and had always had a job since she left school. I hadn't hung out with too many people like her up until then but she quickly made me realise that it was possible to be a strong character and a *good* one at the same time. She lived in Haringey in north London and I started staying with her a lot, away from my normal stomping grounds in the north-west. She told me that if we were going to see each other I would have to get a job. 'I don't want a man who can't pay his way in the world,' she said, and encouraged me to find out about doing some courses at the local college.

It had always been my intention when I was inside to do just that, but, after getting out, moving from a bail hostel in one part of town to another elsewhere hadn't given me much stability or a sound base on which to start building a new life. I began to drift a bit, and it was only meeting Hazel that set me back on the path I had originally intended. I got a place to do a Community Sports Leaders' Award at the College of North East London in Tottenham (or Conel as we knew it), which was the closest suitable college to Hazel's house in Haringey. The course took six months and, after I passed, I enrolled on a more advanced programme called the Hansen Award over a similar period. Once I finished that I took my studies to an even higher level and did a Recreational Management course which was split into two parts, each a year long.

I needed money to pay my way as I studied and, thanks to my friend Paul, I got a job as a forklift truck driver in the warehouse where he worked, even though I had never operated one in my life. After passing an operator's course a few months later, Hazel got me a job in the warehouse attached to the office where she worked in Stratford.

Later, I managed to scrape a job as a lifeguard at the swimming pool in Tottenham Green Leisure Centre – quite an achievement considering I couldn't even swim six weeks earlier. When it came to my test to get the job I could just about do one length of the pool. Unfortunately, I had to do four of them in order to pass and I was almost drowning as I struggled up the final length.

Luckily, there were no dangerous incidents in the pool while I was working there and there were always other guards to help out if there was a problem. All I did was just sit in one of those big chairs looking down on the swimmers or walk around the pool in my shorts and T-shirt with my whistle, stopping people dive-bombing the other swimmers or heavy petting in the pool. I worked on and off at the pool for about three years, alternating between there and the gym, where I worked as a fitness supervisor. After a year, I was able to swim sixty-four lengths non-stop and the swimmers of Tottenham could breathe a sigh of relief.

These were the first real jobs I had had and, although they were only part-time, they earned me a bit of cash while keeping me on the straight and narrow and giving me enough time to go to college and do my homework. But money was still pretty tight, so for a brief period I continued to sign on the dole in Hounslow. However, that deception came to an end pretty quickly when a bloke in the hostel, who used to sign on for me, blew the scam. The guy in the office asked him his name and he gave it to him, to which the guy said, 'Well, then, why are you signing on as Audley?' He was a good bloke, but a bit slow off the mark.

I could no longer afford my £50-a-week rent on the small wages I was earning and there was no more time in the day for me to work because I was studying in the evening. In a very good week during the holidays I would earn about 150 quid, but during term time it was more like half that amount. It was only enough to feed me, pay for transport to college, buy the stationery and so on I needed to study and contribute towards the bills, so I moved in with Hazel. I also found weekend work as a door supervisor (otherwise known as a bouncer) meaning I was busy every day of the week.

I didn't find the studying as hard as I thought it would be after leaving school with no qualifications. I've always been sharp and good with words, even if my grammar left a little to be desired. I was, however, not the most punctual of students or the most conscientious and, despite my determination to get the qualifications, I found the old, lazy, mischief-making Audley was still alive and well. But I got on with my teachers and lecturers at Conel as I was there because I wanted to be, not because I had to be. No one got angry with you if you were late or missed a class. As far as they were concerned, what you did was your decision. It was your life, not theirs, and I liked that respect and did enough work to get by and pass all my exams. I excelled in some modules and even got distinctions and credits, but basically I did what I had to do to get what I wanted and no more.

I also played masses of sport while I was there and even won my first personal sporting award at college– Sports Personality of the Year 1994. I threw myself into everything, just as I had done at school and in prison. I played for the college football, cricket and basketball teams, learned how to swim and worked out in the gym several times a week. Sport, sport, sport – that's all I really wanted to do.

# CHAPTER 3

# LEARNING THE ROPES AT THE SCHOOL OF HARD KNOCKS

It wasn't until I was nineteen years old that I first stepped into a boxing ring. Rodney, my younger brother, was a member of the Northolt boxing club in Rowdell Road, and one night I decided to go and watch him fight in a club competition at Greenford Town Hall. I would be lying if I said that I realised there and then, as I stood in the small crowd cheering on Rodney, that the Virgin Mary appeared before me in a vision and said, 'Audley, you will follow Rodney into the ring and greatness will be bestowed upon you.' It was a bit more prosaic than that, but I liked what I saw enough to go back a couple more times, and when my best friend Paul joined a gym called Middle Row, off Ladbroke Grove, the turning point came. Paul kept trying to persuade me to come down and give it a try, throwing down the challenge that he would mash me up if we sparred with each other. It was an offer I couldn't refuse, and so I went along one evening. I had no preconceptions about whether I would enjoy it or not, or even whether I would be any good or not. I was a good all-round sportsman, but that meant nothing.

I quickly discovered that I was a natural. I was as raw as a boxer can be, but I had an instinctive feel for it: I could throw a natural jab and a natural cross, my movement around the ring and my timing were good, I had quick hands, I could think on my feet – everything felt right, as if I had been boxing for years. I had been a jack of all sporting trades, but after a few evenings in Ladbroke Grove I felt I had found a sport I could master. Once I had started, I couldn't understand how I had never even contemplated taking up boxing in the past. It was so obvious. I had always wanted to achieve fame and success in sport and nothing else really interested me. I was big, powerful and athletic, I was quick on my feet for a man of my size, I had good hand/eye coordination, I loved a scrap, I was more a loner than a team player, and I liked to think of myself as a thinking sportsman rather than a blood-and-thunder hothead. I had all the tools I needed, and during those first weeks in the ring I felt a huge sense of excitement in my stomach.

I made rapid strides and went down to the gym as often as I could. Thanks to Paul, I learned a lot about my potential as a boxer very quickly. He was a light-heavyweight, which meant he was just big enough to be able to spar with me. We were extremely competitive and, each desperate not to be beaten by our best mate, fought ferociously. If I had sparred with anyone else at this time I would probably had been far more cautious, but looking at Paul over the top of my gloves and fearing all the jip he would be giving me if he got the better of me, I tried to knock him to bits.

Around the same time that I took up boxing, I got involved in a street fight with a heavy character, well-known locally, that convinced me I had the courage, the physical tools and the strength of personality to make it. The fight was to become part of west London folklore and over a hundred people turned up to see it: my first fight billed and hyped, I suppose. It took place up in the West End just off Oxford

Street outside a club called Lacy's, where all the 'It' crowd used to go on a Friday night. My opponent, who had a reputation as one of the toughest guys around, was a friend of mine, but when he and two other guys tried to bully Rodney and threatened to beat him up as he sat in his car I wanted revenge.

I was boiling when Rodney told me what had happened, so I challenged the guy to settle it with our fists. It was a matter of family honour and loyalty. The fight was arranged and I rolled up at Lacy's with Paul and a whole gang of my mates, about fifteen of them, all tooled up. He was there waiting with his gang and they were all tooled up too. At first he tried to get out of it, saying he didn't know Rodney was my brother, but then the row quickly escalated and he said, 'So what if he's your fucking brother?'

I said, 'Well, let's go around the corner and I'll show you "So what if he's my fucking brother".'

It was a highly inflammatory situation, and I knew that if I went down I was going to be in big trouble because all hell would have broken loose. And if he had gone down, it would have been the same – either way, the gangs would have piled in. We started going at each other like animals before I managed to knock him down and give him a good hammering, but just as it looked as if the whole situation was about to go off the police came screeching around the corner and everybody, including me, scarpered. No one got caught, but the incident cemented my name in the community as someone not to be messed with. After that night, everyone on the street had heard of Audley Harrison. There was quite a lot of tension for a few months and I knew that some kind of revenge attack was possible, but everything slowly settled down and we became friends again.

When my Dad and brothers jumped me in the street after I had run away from home as a kid and grilled me about what

I was going to do with my life, all I could say was that I knew I was going to be famous. Eight years later, when I was putting on my gloves at Ladbroke Grove I knew I had found the sport which could deliver the fame and success I had predicted and craved. I suppose it is easy for anyone who has achieved some kind of success in their life to look back and claim that they always knew it was going to happen. But – and you can ask anyone in my family or any of my close friends – I always said I was destined to be a star.

I soon joined the Northolt gym, and my first competitive boxing match was on 14 May 1992 against a policeman called Tony Wildgoose in the Top Hat in Ealing. I recall every second of it vividly. Most of the crowd were policemen and I remember thinking what a sweet irony this was – the ex-con has his first fight against the local policeman. I was 'known' to some of the officers in the crowd and I think they saw the funny side of it too. The first round was pretty even, but in the second round I beat him up and the referee stopped the fight. A lot of people might have been jumping around ecstatically after winning their first fight, but I couldn't get back to my corner quick enough. I had trained for months for that evening, but I was still absolutely shattered. I could barely breathe and I just stood there panting – the adrenalin rush of combat had left me drained after no more than five minutes of action. I was hooked. This was sport in its most raw form: two men in direct combat, using all their power and agility and brains to overcome the other. From the moment the referee dragged me off that policeman there was no going back. I would still carry on studying and working to pay my way, but boxing was now a major part of my life.

My second bout, a few weeks later, was even more daunting. I was lined up against this other black fighter from south of the river. I thought it was going to be a war – a turf war transferred to the ring, south London v Harlesden. I got really hyped up and a few of my mates came down to cheer me on. But it turned out to be a farce, as my opponent jumped out of the ring in the first round. He claimed he had walked out in protest at the referee, who kept warning him for holding me, but I thought he might be frightened he was going to take a beating.

My third fight took place in the East Ham Working Men's Club, a really old-fashioned boxing venue with a permanent smell of fags, beer and sweat. This was going to be an entirely different and tougher encounter from my last. The guy I was fighting was called Steve Cranston, a huge bloke, even bigger than me. He had a reputation as a hardman in and out of the ring, and the last I heard he had been locked away for about ten years. When I walked into the gym and saw the guy I thought, 'Oh, cheers. Thanks for putting me up against this monster in just my third fight.' My record was 2–0 (two wins, no defeats) and his was 4–0 with a couple of knockouts. I was as nervous as I had ever been, because I knew he could cause some damage. He was from the east and I was from the west, and to some extent we were representing our neighbourhoods. When the fight began we shadowed each other around the ring before I threw a one-two. The right jab missed but my left cross was straight down the pipe, bang on the chin, and he crumpled like a paper bag.

It was a strange experience. I was buzzing so much with nerves and adrenalin that I had zoned out and was fighting on automatic pilot, unaware of what I was doing. Now I understand what was happening: in sports psychology, they call this sensation 'flow'. It's not quite an out-of-body experience, but you feel like a puppet with some other force pulling the strings. This fight was another important milestone for me because it made me realise I could perform under pressure. I had always thought nerves could only be a negative thing that impaired your judgement and undermined your courage. But this fight showed me that nerves can even be a help, as they heighten your senses and make you more alert.

Pat Wilson, my trainer at Northolt, told me afterwards that he was genuinely worried for me before I went into the ring that night. I was a virtual novice, nothing like as strong as I am now, and I was fighting a guy with arms as thick as his legs. Pat said he even contemplated not watching because he didn't want to see me get flattened. He said he couldn't believe it when my opponent hit the canvas so hard – he thought the ring was going to collapse. Pat Wilson was a good man and a very good trainer for me in those early days, and I'll always be grateful for his help. (On the day I arrived back from Sydney after the Olympics I was touched to see his face in the crowd to welcome me home.)

My first competitive fight in the new season – my fourth in total – was against another policeman called Danny Hopkins. It took place in Finchley on a Friday, and I beat him on points in a tough fight. The following morning I woke up with a bit of flu, but I thought nothing of it until the following Tuesday when the Northolt people told me I had been challenged to a rematch at a hotel in Crystal Palace against the bloke from south London who had jumped out of the ring in my second fight. He said he wanted to fight me again to prove that the first fight was a non-contest because of the referee. By the night of the fight my flu was full-blown and I was feeling really low and lacking in energy. I had aches and pains all over my body and the last thing I felt like doing was going into the ring and getting hit. My head was hurting enough just when I sneezed, and God knows how I would feel having my head and body worked over by Mr Angry from south London.

The situation got even worse when we arrived at Crystal Palace that evening and the guy I was up against went down with a bad back and couldn't fight. I was feeling so poorly that

I was quite relieved when I heard the fight was off – until they added they had arranged for a replacement. It all seemed a bit suspicious, and I felt I had been stitched up when they told me that the guy I would now be fighting was called Keith Long, a really good fighter who is now a pro and who had won all four of his amateur bouts with knockouts. I suspected that the organisers of the show just wanted me mashed up and humiliated. They had got me on to the card and knew I couldn't now say I wasn't fighting this guy. I would have lost face, and they would have gone away and told everyone I was chicken. So we fought, and the bout went the full three rounds. We were both working each other really hard, and it was anyone's fight until late in the last round when I got him with a massive left in his belly and that was it. It completely took the wind out of him and for the rest of the round I was all over him and took the fight on points.

A couple of months later I had a rematch with the policeman Danny and stopped him with a cut in the second round. That made it six wins out of six (or 'six and O' as they say on the circuit). I then had a long stretch with no fights because I couldn't get on the card of any club shows. There weren't a lot of super-heavyweights around at the time. There are always a lot of boxers around on the lighter weights, but super-heavyweights are a less common breed. There was also the problem of my perfect record – guys with only a couple of fights under their belts didn't want to run the risk of getting beaten so early in their amateur career. So I found myself in limbo. I wanted a few more fights on the club circuit to toughen me up for greater challenges, and, being a late-comer to boxing, I was probably still a bit too raw to move up a level and start challenging for the national Amateur Boxing Association of England (ABA) titles. So I entered The Novice Championships, but again there was either no one in my weight or my opponents pulled out and I ended up winning the final on a walkover.

As the months wore on and no fights were forthcoming, Pat Wilson decided there was no choice but to throw me in at the deep end. It was almost unheard of for a boxer to enter the ABAs after just six competitive bouts, but my career was going nowhere and we had to take action. After just two years or so as a boxer I found myself in the ring against England's top amateur performers. I would experience some great highs over those next few years, but also some very bad lows. I have no regrets about this period, even though my amateur record suffered badly at the beginning, because the experience on the ABA circuit helped me grow up very fast. It was a very steep upward learning curve and I was just a rookie starting at the bottom. All my technical, tactical and physical weaknesses were exposed at some time or other, and I was able to go away and work on them. I also learned that the right mental and physical preparation would be vital if I was going to make it to the top. I couldn't just swagger into the ring and expect my natural ability and aggression to carry me to victory.

But after three hard years I would be able to consider myself a genuinely world-class performer. I suffered a number of setbacks on the way, but I turned those experiences into something positive and by the time I went to the 1998 Commonwealth Games I knew as much about the science and psychology of boxing as any amateur in the country. Critics have looked at my record over that period and said, 'Well, the guy can't be that good.' In reply, I would say that I took the hard road at a time when I was nowhere near ready for that level, technically or psychologically, but each time I was knocked back I responded by picking myself up and analysing what had gone wrong. I could have been overwhelmed by it all and given up, but I didn't: it just made me more determined to succeed. I hold up my Commonwealth and Olympic gold medals as glittering proof that, in the end, my perseverance and determination paid off. If anything, the way I responded showed my strength of character as much as it showed any weakness in my technique and preparations.

The London ABA area is split into four regional divisions, and I had to win the North West division in order to have a crack at the London title. If you win your division you go into London semis and then to the final, then on to the national quarters, semis and the final. In my first season there was no one to fight in the North West division and I got a bye straight into the London semis, which also featured Julius Francis, who was outright favourite for the national title that year, and a guy called Tom Cheribim from the Repton Boys' Club in the East End. Both of them were seasoned, highly respected boxers and Francis, the number one ranked amateur at the time, would soon turn professional and become British heavy-weight champion and even land a fight against Mike Tyson. There were only three of us that year because there was no one put forward from the South West division, and when the draw was made it was me who got the bye to the final and they had to fight each other in the only semi. Julius came over to me after the draw, grinning from ear to ear, slapped me on the back and said, 'Look forward to seeing you in the final, Audley.'

He was as good as his word and knocked out Tom Cheribim, but immediately people started saying that the final shouldn't take place because of fears for my safety. I was a six-fight novice, the outright underdog, while he was widely regarded as the best amateur super-heavyweight in the country. The local papers and the boxing rags all predicted that I was going to be knocked out in the first round. But I was determined to make a fight of it and show that, despite being just a kid in terms of boxing experience, I had the potential and the heart to succeed against the best. In a way it was a no-lose situation for me, because no one gave me a prayer – even I didn't know what I was capable of achieving. Fighting someone of Julius' calibre would provide me with a good benchmark of my potential and my progress so far.

Despite all the protests the fight went ahead – and it was close, far closer than anyone had dared predict. I think even my own camp were a little apprehensive before the bout. In all my other fights, Pat had just put on my headguard before the start but on this occasion he wrapped tape around it. Pat was obviously really worried for me going in there with Julius, but his precautions hardly filled me with confidence. It went the distance, and Julius edged it on points. One judge gave it to me and the other two to him, but all the decisions were tight. As the fight went on I grew in confidence. He took the first round but the second was pretty even and in the last I was on top of him, no doubt about it, and I thought I had done enough to swing it in my favour. I remember the crowd getting behind me as they sensed an upset and that gave me a real lift. Far from being overwhelmed, I was enjoying every moment of it. There I was against the favourite for the national title and I was giving him a run for his money, getting stronger and stronger by the final bell. I was upset that the decision went against me but at the same time I felt proud that I had acquitted myself so well after several months without a competitive fight. Sparring is one thing, but in no way can it prepare you for the challenge of real competition. You're on your own then: just you and your opponent, with your reputations and careers and pride at stake, going hell for leather at each other with the adrenalin rush that comes from combat squeezing the breath out of your lungs.

The Francis fight was my first ever defeat, and it sits on my record as plain as day for everyone to see. But I actually took a lot of pride from the way I performed that night against one of Britain's best super-heavyweights of the 1990s.

After the fight, I stopped training as I thought my ABA challenge for that season was over, but a few weeks later there was a dramatic development. Two days before his national quarter final contest, Julius was caught fighting on an unlicensed show, something which he used to do quite regularly. He was immediately banned from going any further in the national championships and subsequently turned professional; the organisers then asked me, as his opponent in the London final, to take his place in the national quarters. There were more concerns raised about the wisdom of letting me fight because I was so inexperienced, but Tom Cheribim was ruled out because Julius had knocked him out and he was on an automatic twenty-eight-day lay-off period.

With hindsight I shouldn't have accepted, because I wasn't in the right mental or physical condition. It's important to be in a good frame of mind for a fight, and you only get that from the momentum generated in the build-up to it. By the time the fight comes around you should be coming to the boil physically and mentally, like a sprung coil to be unleashed on your opponent. But if you literally pick yourself off the sofa, grab your kit bag and turn up at the venue you are starting with a serious disadvantage. That's what happened to me when I stupidly accepted the offer to fight Rod Allen in the last eight of the national competition. I already had the Julius Francis defeat against my name, and at that early stage of my career I shouldn't have run the risk of registering another loss on my record. Rod Allen was a big, strong guy from up north but he was nothing exceptional and I was still a bit happy-go-lucky in those days and thought I could waltz in there. Wisdom comes from experience, and I certainly felt a bit wiser after the fight. I put in a flat performance. I just wasn't in shape and didn't have the tools to do the job, and he beat me on points.

If anything good came out of my first year on the ABA circuit, it was that I had exposed myself to the highest level of amateur boxing in the country and learned some hard lessons about the importance of preparation. I had lost two fights but I knew that, with better training, I could be challenging and beating these guys in the near future. I was a little rash in my haste to get on, a little casual in my preparations and a little naïve in the way I walked blindly into important fights. In the past I had always managed to transform adversity into something that could work to my advantage, and that is exactly what I intended to do now. The plan was to spend 1993 getting as many club fights as possible before having another shot at the ABA national title in the 1993–94 season. But once again it was proving impossible to get any bouts and so I was forced to enter the ABAs again even though I had been completely inactive for months.

I won the North West London divisional title after two fights and then won the semis to make it to the final, where I would face a Chechen dental student called Mohammed Khamkoer. People knew very little about him except that he had been brought over here to further his studies and joined a local club, Fitzroy Lodge. The novelty of having a non-Englishman fighting for the English title prompted a fair amount of media interest, mainly in the local London press and the boxing papers but also some in the national papers. Reading the articles, we quickly discovered that this guy was more than a bit experienced and had made something of a name for himself back home before coming to England. I knew I was going to be in for another tough fight, but in the first round he didn't do much to scare me. He had this horrible, gangly style which slightly put me off, but apart from that he didn't look like he was going to cause me that much bother.

At the start of the second I was quietly confident and threw out a big left which half caught him, but as I opened myself up to hit him I was slightly off balance and he caught me with a big left hook on the chin and threw me against the ropes. It completely stunned me and I vaguely remember just leaning on the ropes trying to stay on my feet, spitting out and thinking that all my teeth had been shattered (by a trainee dentist). The referee started the count on me and, although I felt groggy, I was basically OK to continue. Another ten seconds or so and the fog would have lifted, and I said to the match referee, 'I'm all right ref, I'm fine.' But he counted me out and that was that – my ABA dream was over for another year. It was the only time in my career I have been counted out, and I was gutted at the time.

I was entering the lowest ebb of my boxing career, and my ABA setback was not the only cause for gloom. At around this time I was sounded out about boxing for Jamaica in the 1994 Commonwealth Games in Canada, and I got in touch with the relevant authorities. (My defeat by Khamkoer had ended any distant hopes I had of representing England out there.) They agreed to pick me and said they would pay my way, but after it was announced there was a major outcry in Jamaica about me representing them because I hadn't boxed in their national championships; people said I was just jumping on a bandwagon to further my career. Money – as always – was at the heart of the problem. Some of the other athletes said they were annoyed that I would be getting Jamaican funds, which were even tighter than here in England.

The Jamaican officials came to a compromise, saying I could go but only if I paid my own way. A media campaign was launched in the black press and the *Hackney Gazette* to help me raise some money, but we couldn't raise enough and I eventually scrapped the whole plan – thank God. I think it would have been a disaster if I had gone, because I would have been annihilated out there. I was nowhere near ready for that level, as my ABA experience had shown.

The Jamaica incident was another example of how I was suffering at the hands of my own over-enthusiasm and naïvety at this time. In boxing I had finally found a way of making a potential success of myself and I was in a hurry to get on with my career. It wasn't just that I was a late-comer to the sport and was trying to cram as much in as possible – more that I was over-excited by it all, like a kid in a sweetshop who wants everything at once. That year was an object lesson in how not to go about an early career in amateur boxing, and I still shudder to think about the consequences had I represented Jamaica in Canada. It could have killed my amateur career – and thus my professional career – stone dead. You don't get a second chance at that level. Four years later, I represented England in the Commonwealth Games in Kuala Lumpur and returned with the gold medal around my neck. It was that success which launched my Olympic dream, which in turn led to my career as a professional. Almost certainly none of that would have happened if I had fought for Jamaica in 1994, and I suppose I might even have given up the sport altogether and just concentrated on my studies.

Thinking about the Jamaica experience now, it makes me realise that a career in boxing is like walking a tightrope – one major wobble and you will be sent plunging headlong. It is vital to have a good team around from the earliest possible stage – a team of wise, experienced people who know all the pitfalls that lie in the path of the boxer. I am sure there are hundreds of ex-boxers in Britain – and elsewhere for that matter – who are now working as labourers or in an office, as well as quite a few in prison, but who could have tasted success at the highest level had they been brought on in the right way.

I had considered fighting for Jamaica because my West Indian roots are very important to me. I am a Brent-born Brit of Jamaican parents, ultimately of African descent, and so I feel rooted in a number of traditions. I am proud of being a London boy, I am proud of being British, and I am proud of my Jamaican and African heritage. Roots are important: they ground you and give you your basic bearings as to who you are. A man is allowed more than one cause to champion in his life, and I think it's possible to be proud of different traditions at the same time. Just because I am a proud Briton doesn't mean I can't also be proud of Jamaica. Take, for example, the guy who goes to cheer his local amateur football team one day, then goes off to support Chelsea, his club team, a few days later, then England or Wales or Scotland in the rugby internationals, then the whole of Great Britain at the Olympics, then Europe in the Ryder Cup and so on. . . . There is no limit to our potential allegiances. I feel lucky that I have so many reasons to be proud. I don't feel confused or feel my loyalties pulled in different directions. I think it boils down to having pride in yourself, and then it follows logically that you will be proud of all your traditions.

It was around this time that I became interested in sports psychology. I had heard about sports psychology from my studies, but had never taken it that seriously. I had always believed that the only person who could help a sportsman was himself, and that the only mental tools he needed to succeed were self-belief and his own sheer bloody-minded determination to win. I had this idea fixed in my mind that if I went to a psychologist he would ask me to lie down on his couch and tell him about my childhood. Then he would tell me that the reason why my left jab wasn't working was because my Dad took away my bag of sherbet bon-bons when I was five. But after the setbacks over the last few months I wanted as much help and advice as I could get to help lift my game to a higher level, and after a couple of guys in the gym told me they had been to sports psychologists and found the experience really beneficial I decided it to give it a go. I only had a couple of sessions with a man called Jack Mitchell, whose ad I saw in one of the boxing magazines, but it was enough to open my eyes to the importance of the mental aspect of an athlete's training. I was unable to afford regular sessions with Jack at the time, but at least he got me thinking.

Feeling a bit disillusioned and down on myself at the end of the 1994 season, I allowed myself to get out of condition. A few weeks into the summer I was phoned up and asked to box for a London select team at a meeting in Trondheim in Norway. Stupidly, I agreed. I thought the trip might be a bit of fun, as well as giving me a break from London and helping me to forget about the last, frustrating couple of months. I had a great time out there – we met some nice Norwegian girls and it was a bit of a party, to be honest – but from a boxing point of view it was another step backwards. I was badly out of shape and in my only fight I was rubbish while some nobody just worked me over like I was his punch bag. I was really flat-footed and it felt like I was wearing concrete ski boots. It was the fourth defeat of my fledgling career. A few months earlier my record had been 6–0, now it was 8–4. My reputation had slid from that of an outstanding talent to a mediocrity because I had not yet learned to say no to anyone or how to manage my career intelligently. On the plane back to London, I made up my mind that I would stop drifting as a boxer. No more naïve decisions, no more casual preparation. It was time to get serious about my career or to forget the whole thing and concentrate on my studies and earning some money.

I returned to competitive action in 1995 a far wiser, sharper and fitter boxer than I had finished the last. I spent a lot of time in the gym, working out to keep in shape so I could hit the ground running when the new campaign began.

Before the ABA national championships got under way I boxed a guy called Harry Senior on a club show. Harry was one of the best amateurs around at the time and had beaten Danny Williams in the South West London division finals. It was after that defeat that Danny turned pro. I annihilated Harry in this fight, totally took him to school. I was skilful and powerful and was all over him for the whole contest. It was probably my classiest fight up to that point and gave me a huge lift, helping to wipe out some of my disappointment from the end of last season and raising my confidence that I was starting to come of age. I had also put some red tassels on my boots and got some flashy blue shorts, both of which, in their own little way, encouraged me to be a bit stylish and flamboyant in the ring.

Over the summer I had decided I needed a change of direction, a fresh challenge. I had been at Northolt for four years and loved every moment of it, made some great friends and will always be grateful to the people, especially Pat Wilson, who helped set me on the road in the boxing world. But I had grown stale and needed to be pushed harder, so I decided to move to the Repton Boys' Club in Bethnal Green, which, apart from being easier to get to from Haringey, was also one of the best set-ups in town. I couldn't get regular sparring partners at Northolt, but at Repton I thought that wouldn't be a problem. I knew there were a lot of top fighters there and a lot of guys with big attitude. That was exactly what I needed, having drifted a bit into the comfort zone in Northolt and got punished for it in the ring. At Repton I hoped to moved up to a much higher level of boxing. A lot of good fighters had trained there, including ten former Olympians.

My first spell at Repton didn't last very long. In fact it lasted about half an hour. I walked into the gym and told this young trainer that my name was Audley Harrison and I would like to speak to Tony Burns, the head trainer, about joining the gym. This guy pretended that he didn't know who I was and started giving me some serious attitude. He saw my mobile phone and asked, 'Are you a drug dealer or something? Most of you black guys from Hackney are.' The guy was just trying to wind me up – as they always do at Repton I would discover later – but as I stood there listening to this guy mouthing off at me, I said, 'Forget it mate' and just walked out the door and joined the Islington gym a couple of miles up the road. The move turned out to be a painful leap from the frying pan into the fire. When I got there I found that most of the top super-heavyweights had left: some had turned pro in America, some had left for other gyms and some had stopped boxing altogether. I found myself in exactly the same situation as I had been at Northolt towards the end of my time there. I was all revved up, with no one to fight. To compound the problem – and perhaps as a result of my general frustration – I got on even worse with the people there than with those at Repton, and especially badly with the guy who ran the gym. He was an old-school disciplinarian and I didn't agree with a lot of his ideas. We just didn't hit it off as personalities and had a load of flare-ups. By this stage, I was beginning to wonder if I was ever going to get a break. In career terms I had had a miserable time of it and was determined to start all over again with a fresh attitude, but the Islington experience was depressing. I had taken decisive action by leaving my first club, Northolt, to go there, but didn't enjoy it at all. I decided that I would stick it out for the season, fight for the ABA titles, and then move on at the end of the season.

The 1995 season at Islington was a difficult one in many ways but I still managed to produce some of my best boxing yet. Once again I won the North West London title, stopping a guy in the second round. In the London semis I looked sensational and destroyed this guy called Jamie Beercroft. My confidence came flooding back and I felt I could take on anyone. In the London final, my third in a row, I was up against Harry Senior, whom I had bashed up in a club show at the start of the season, and it was a similar story this time round. I was working the ring so well that he could barely get near me, and I destroyed him on points. At long last, London Champion at my third attempt – my first milestone.

I was drawn against a soldier called Danny Watts in the national quarters. Watts was undoubtedly one of the best super-heavyweights in the country at the time, and had lost to Danny Williams in a box-off to decide who would represent England at the Commonwealth Games. The fight, which took place in the army barracks in Aldershot, turned out to be one I quickly wanted to forget. Watts was clear favourite to win, and I have to confess that for the first and only time in my career I felt fazed about a fight. It wasn't so much the prospect of facing him in the ring, but the whole day was weird and slightly disturbing from the moment we arrived. There were soldiers in uniform everywhere, doing drill on the parade ground or dressed up in combat gear ready to head off on exercise. There were bands playing regimental tunes, and everywhere I walked I could hear drum rolls. It felt like I was about to fight the whole of the British Army. It wasn't me against Danny Watts, but me against every squaddie in the country.

A lot of my friends had come down to support me, including Hazel, my best friend Paul and his girlfriend, and we were all slightly overwhelmed by the bizarre environment. This was a world a million miles away from the streets of Haringey and Harlesden, and we had never come across anything quite like it. We wandered around for a while, then decided to get away for a while and drove into town. We all crammed into the car and went and grabbed a takeaway. To cut a long story short, I was a long way from being in the right state of mind when I walked through a crowd of squaddies for the fight. I had never come across Danny Watts, but when I stepped into the ring I just saw this big white guy in the other corner, bigger than me, and he looked like a Rottweiler who had not eaten for a week. He was virtually frothing at the mouth and snarling, and I could tell he was just going to throw himself from the first bell, roared on by all his mates.

As I looked at him, straining on his leash in the corner, I thought, 'What's my game plan?' and realised I didn't have one. I had come tactically and mentally ill-equipped and, as I suspected, he came at me from the off. There was no cautious build-up in his approach – he just jumped on me and started working me all over my body. Early on he caught me with a big left hook flush on the chin, and from then on it was a matter of survival. No exaggeration, I felt like I was fighting for my life in there. I was groggy from the left hook and could not think clearly enough to come up with a strategy to get out of trouble.

When the blows are flying in, you're punch-drunk, your heart is beating out of control and the adrenalin is surging through your body, you just feel completely disorientated, like you are on some scary fairground ride which you cannot stop. I couldn't wait for the bell at the end of the first and when it came I sat in my corner, panting like an old Labrador who had just run to Aldershot from Harlesden. But the break allowed me to get my breath back and gather my composure. In the second round I started to give him a half-decent fight, but he still had the better of it. The fight was only three rounds and I knew he had won on points and my chances of making the semis had gone, and in the third I knew I had to knock him out. If I could not do that I at least wanted to restore a bit of my pride and I did to some extent, although overall he was still very much the deserved winner. It was the worst mauling I have ever taken in the ring and gave me lots to think about on our very silent drive back to London. I realised I had lost the fight before it had begun. I had been fazed by the surroundings and had responded negatively to the situation. I realised I couldn't just casually roll up for a big fight with a bunch of mates, walk around town, eat a burger and then get into a ring against one of the best amateurs around and expect to leave the place victorious. This was another important milestone in Audley Harrison's steep learning curve.

Realising that my mental preparation had been seriously wrong, one of the first things I did on my return to London was immerse myself in the science of sports psychology. I learned a whole number of important things about mental preparation during the build-up to a fight, but there were one or two techniques that I found particularly beneficial and still use today as part of my programme. I learned to relax and harness my nervous energy to my advantage and channel it to a positive end. But perhaps most importantly I learned a very useful technique called 'visualisation', which sounds a bit academic but is actually a pretty straightforward procedure.

What you do is literally visualise the upcoming fight, imagining exactly what you want to do in the fight itself. I found it really helpful, because what I was doing was almost pre-programming myself and making me more methodical and thoughtful in the ring. Visualisation gives you great confidence because you know you have a clear game plan mapped out in your head in vivid images. Of course, it is not a watertight process with a hundred per cent success rate because the direction and nature of a fight are often driven by events on the canvas and you cannot predict with exact accuracy how your opponent is going to approach the fight. But by watching videos beforehand or simply knowing about a boxer's style you can obtain a pretty fair idea of how your opponent is going to fight. Even if the fight does not go exactly as you visualised it, you can prepare yourself by visualising a number of alternatives which allow you to adapt. They are your contingency plans, so if Plan A is not on the cards visualisation allows you to change tack in mid-fight.

Visualisation is only a part of your total preparation, but it helped to avoid a repeat of the situation I found myself in against Danny Watts when I had little or no idea about how to outbox him tactically. Guts and physical power and skill are obviously the main weapons of the boxer, but thinking on your feet and sound mental and tactical preparation are also vital. When Muhammad Ali beat George Foreman in the Rumble in the Jungle, he beat him with his head as much as with his fists. Foreman pummelled him and pummelled him and Ali just sat on the ropes, taking all the punishment, and then when Foreman had burned up every last ounce of energy trying to overwhelm him with brute force, Ali just came off the ropes and cleaned up. It was a stunning display of tactics, based on a big gamble that he could take the battering. Ali, of course, needed the physical strength to withstand the bombardment in the first place, but he obviously knew that he didn't have the tools to match Foreman in the power department, so he used his brain to win the fight. I don't know whether it was pre-planned strategy or whether, once in the ring and feeling the force of Foreman's blows, he decided there and then to take that tactical route, but either way he outfoxed Foreman.

My study of sports psychology helped me improve my own state of mind before and during a fight as well as in a more general sense. I set myself clear goals for the coming years: first to win the national ABA title and then the Commonwealth Games gold in Kuala Lumpur. I wanted to narrow my focus and put out of my mind, as best I could, all those wilder ambitions and dreams about Olympic titles, world heavyweight championship fights, beating Tyson at a packed Wembley, becoming famous, earning serious money for myself and my family. As a result, I became much more intense in everything that I did. From now on, I was going to take it one careful step at a time. Before, I had been so unfocused I was like a blunderbuss, spraying myself in all directions, but I was beginning to develop a cannier, more scientific streak.

It was with my tail firmly between my legs that I returned to Repton and spoke to Tony Burns about joining. Repton, I was to learn very quickly, is a great gym. They will do whatever it takes to make you a better boxer, whether that means throwing you out on the street to make you learn a lesson about attitude or giving you financial assistance.

The gym, formerly the Bethnal Green public baths, is one of the most famous amateur clubs in the country, once used by Ronnie and Reggie Kray, and actors Ray Winstone and Glen Murphy. More recently, several scenes from the gangster movie *Lock, Stock and Two Smoking Barrels* were filmed there. Repton's philosophy was to become mine: do things properly or don't do them at all. Tony Burns is a craggy-faced haulage company owner with a big passion for Repton and amateur boxing as a whole. He has spent thirty years, nearly half his life, at the club and has no time for prima donnas and bigheads. He is said to have once thrown out the Krays after rumours they were using the gym to hire henchmen. He'll coming wandering into the gym, fag hanging out of his mouth, and straightaway he'll be taking the piss and putting you on the back foot. But you have to look beyond the surface of the character, learn how to handle him, and recognise that he has got a whole lot of knowledge and experience to pass on. I realised after a few weeks that there was far more to the man than his manner might suggest at first. His great strength is that he makes you think for yourself. He doesn't molly-cuddle you, but inspires you to start working out your own strengths and weaknesses. He'd be the first person to have a laugh at you if you got knocked out, but he is a master of psychological games. 'You're not seriously going to let this guy piss all over you, are you, Audley?' he would say in the corner at the end of a round you thought you had won. He would give you confidence, but in an unorthodox way.

The only criticism levelled at Repton is that it doesn't produce champions – it just takes the most talented boxers from elsewhere. But the fact is that year after year Repton does produce champions and Tony Burns is a first-class coach. Perhaps one of the reasons that a lot of top amateurs go there is because they know they are going to get looked after, which is not something you can say about every gym in the country.

# CHAPTER 4

# AN ALL-ROUND EDUCATION

Throughout this period I was fighting a protracted legal battle with the Commissioner of the Police for the Metropolis for financial compensation after an incident with the police.

In May 1993, Hazel and I went to Stoke Newington Police station wishing to make a statement to a senior officer about the arrest of a man in the street. We didn't know the man but we believed he had been mistreated by some officers. A senior officer was unwilling to take our statement and when we expressed our intention to go to another station to file our complaint, we were prevented from leaving the station by officers who committed assaults against us. We were both then falsely imprisoned.

Hazel and I were injured in the assaults to the extent that we required medical attention. We were kept, unlawfully, in the station for about seven hours. The final insult occurred when Hazel was charged with assault and I was charged with obstructing the Inspector in the execution of his duty. Hazel was absolutely distraught about the prospect of going to court as she has never been in trouble with the law. She ended up suffering from post traumatic stress disorder.

After the incident we made contact with a pressure group called the Hackney Defence Association, who campaign against police brutality. They were a great help. Through them we contacted Vicky Guedalla (of Dieghton & Guedalla) who had dealt with numerous cases like this and with their support, Hazel was able to feel more positive about the outcome of the case.

We finally stood trial on the 17 September 1993. The stipendiary magistrate dismissed all charges against us, citing inconsistencies in the officers' statements as a reason for concern.

The case attracted a lot of publicity and through Vicky we launched a civil action against the police for false imprisonment, assault and battery, and malicious prosecution. As is the norm with these cases, the Commissioner denied responsibility. He repeated that the officers stood by their statements, but the fact that we attended the police station in good faith as concerned members of the public, and had to endure violent arrests and the deprivation of our liberty without cause, which could have led to a wrongful conviction had the officers' evidence been believed, meant financial compensation was likely. Without admission of any liability the Commissioner agreed to settle the case by paying me £27,500 and Hazel £35,000 plus our legal costs. This was agreed almost six years after the incident.

As with most things in life, what goes around always comes around. One of the main culprits involved in our case, PC Paul Evans, was later found guilty at the Old Bailey of assaulting some other innocent member of the public and given a custodial sentence. I sincerely hope his time inside was made very difficult by the inmates.

The memories of this episode will stay with me forever,

along with the scar on my right wrist from the handcuffs, but through our perseverance and a good solicitor, justice was done. People ask me how I view the police today in the light of that experience, and I still feel uncomfortable that large amounts of tax payers' money is paid out to settle claims but no one accepts responsibility for the action of the officers. With authority comes accountability and I find it unacceptable that certain officers can abuse their positions and hide behind the veil of the law.

The police do a good job overall and I for one realise the importance of a police force to control and maintain order, but every single officer has to know that the force will punish them if they choose to break the law and abuse their positions.

I had to take the whole of the 1996 season off after undergoing my first of three hernia operations. The operation was not a great success as the staples they inserted literally grated on my nerves and required a second, corrective operation at the end of 1997. Still the problem wouldn't clear up and I was forced to carry the injury through the 1998 Commonwealth Games. It was so bad that if if I did more than 30-sit-ups the hernia would start spasming. I had a third operation after the Games and, touch wood, the problem seems to have been rectified.

Being told I needed an operation in 1996 was a major blow, as my career was interrupted at a crucial time. I had taken on board all the lessons learned from my run of defeats, locating the weaknesses in my game, and I was desperate to prove myself at the highest amateur level. During my enforced lay-off, I just concentrated on keeping as fit as possible while focusing on my studies. On the back of my qualifications gained at the College of North East London I had won a place at Brunel University, which was then based in Isleworth, Middlesex, in 1994. I had actually applied for a place the year before and although I could have got in because I was 'county' standard at boxing, I was advised to go back to Conel for another year so that I would be more experienced academically.

My degree was in Sports Studies and Leisure Management and I was at the university for a total of four years, rather than the normal three, because my boxing commitments, particularly in the run-up to the Commonwealth Games, meant that I was unable to give my studies my full attention and I had to do an extra year.

I was very busy during my whole time at university. Just studying for a degree can be a full-time occupation as there is no limit to the amount of work you can put into it. But I was also boxing and training as much as possible, first to try and win the ABA national title, then in preparation for the Commonwealth Games, then the World Championships. I was also working here and there to try and earn some cash and stop my overdraft from spiralling out of control.

While I was at Brunel I revamped the university boxing club, which had fallen on hard times and had basically stopped running. There was a punch bag in the gym and that was about it, so I decided to do something about it. Money, of course, was the problem and I had to persuade the Student Union to release some of their precious funds to help us get up and running and then to pay the ongoing administrative costs. My courses at Conel and my degree studies had taught me a lot about how to run an organisation on a day-to-day basis, keeping the books up to date and setting up committees. I had also completed a four-month aerobics course at Morley College in Lambeth, which qualified me as an instructor, and I wanted to introduce boxercise and show how the club could also be a vehicle for fitness training.

At first the Union were pretty reluctant and said the money should go to what they saw as more worthwhile pursuits. It's strange how many people are prejudiced about boxing and

believe it is a barbaric practice with no place in a civilised society, and it's even stranger how you never hear anyone who
has boxed say this. More often than not, the people who
promote this view have absolutely no idea about the true
nature of the sport. For a start, no one makes boxers box. They
do it because they want to. It is their choice and their right as
individuals in a free society to do as they see fit. It is not for
meddling outsiders to decide what is good for other people
and it is insulting to claim to know better than the boxers
themselves what is or isn't good for them. If the critics don't
want to box, that's fine, but let others do as they please. I felt
so strongly about the worthiness of amateur boxing (and still
do) that I wrote a ten thousand-word thesis for my degree
entitled 'A Sociological Perspective on the Justification of
Amateur Boxing'. Amateur boxing is also a safe sport: you
wear headgear, and there have been very few tragedies in the
amateur ring. It has been said so often already that it should
almost be needless to point it out these days, but there are
many more dangerous sports and pursuits than amateur
boxing: horse riding, motor racing, sailing and almost all
outdoor adventure pursuits like mountaineering and rock
climbing.

Amateur boxing also provides young males with an outlet
for their natural aggression and teaches them the virtues of
discipline and respect for others. To say it saves kids from the
ghetto is a bit of an oversimplification, but it is certainly true
that boxers are far less likely to cause trouble out on the street
than kids hanging around with nothing to do and with no
outlet for their energies and frustrations. I've never felt happy
with this idea of 'boxing out of the ghetto' because it gives the
impression that a boxer has nothing going for him apart from
his fists. It is a stereotype and a cliché that implies that boxers
are just thick bad boys who have battered their way to a more
'respectable' world. Boxers are no more and no less intelligent

than other sportsmen or than most other people in different walks of life. Perhaps because it appears to be such a physical sport, people assume that you don't need a brain to do it. Funny how no one tried telling Muhammad Ali that. Boxing is not a dumb man's sport.

Eventually, I managed to persuade the Brunel Student Union that amateur boxing was a good cause and they put up the cash to help us get started. One of the biggest fears in student unions with responsibility for big sums of money is that there are a lot of freeloaders around who just want money for nothing. Most students are more than a little tight for cash, and unions insist that every last penny they hand out is accounted for. I wanted to prove to Brunel that the boxing club was not on the make and that we were very serious about what we were doing. From the outset, I was meticulous about keeping every receipt and detailing every item of expenditure in our budget, and after the first year I think they were impressed by our efficiency.

The club was a huge success. At the beginning there were just a handful of guys into boxing, but within a year we had about forty regulars and I set up a dedicated boxing gym with all the right equipment and facilities. About seven of them reached such a good level that I was able to get them regis- tered with the Amateur Boxing Association and took them out to fight on club shows. At the same time I did the governing body's assistant coaching course and obtained the certificate which allowed me to train these guys and take them off to those shows. Having left school with no qualifications, I now seemed to be accumulating them for fun. At the time it felt like I was living ten people's lives at once. I had always been an active person, but now all my energies were being chan- nelled into these specific challenges. My feet barely touched the ground during this time, although I still made sure that I saw my mates at the weekend when I would go back to north-west London or into the West End where I worked as a door supervisor.

I was a mature student at Brunel, and by that I don't mean I grew a beard, wore edible sandals and bothered the undergraduate girls at the Student Union disco. But I had already seen a lot of life and I didn't do all the things that most students normally do like lie around drinking lager, smoking pot and watching Ceefax because they can't be bothered to get off their beds. I didn't need to do the sex, drugs and rock'n'roll thing – or the lie-around-in-a-coma thing – because I had done all that since I was about twelve and had grown out of it. I was also about eight years older than most of the students there, and the people I trained and boxed with at the university club looked up to me as a sort of agony uncle whom they could come to if they were having problems. They all knew I had been around the block a few times and could probably give them some sensible advice based on my personal experiences in life. I am still in touch with a lot of them now.

Lots of other students started to come and the club slowly became a significant part of life on the campus. After I won the gold medal at the Commonwealth Games, the interest in it grew even greater because I became a role model to others. They realised that ours was not just some parochial little club, and that it was possible to have ambitions well beyond the four walls of that gym.

It was so successful that I felt confident enough to stage an invitational competition, for which boxers from seven other universities entered. It was like *University Challenge* with fists, and it probably marked the high point of the club. For all other sports there was a national competition overseen by BUSA (British Universities Sports Association), but in this year they had decided to ban boxing from the competition. I contacted them and tried to persuade them that what they had done was unfair, but in the end I decided to press ahead regardless and organise a competition under the auspices of the ABA and following their rules governing medical supervision and so on.

It took a lot of organisation to make it happen and there was a lot of politics involved with all the different boxing bodies, the Health and Safety people and so on, but we finally got it up and running and on the night it went down brilliantly. Each of the universities had their own group of supporters and cheered on their boxers, and at the end we had a big party. Running the club demanded a lot of my time, on top of studying and my boxing commitments outside of the university, but I feel very proud of what we achieved.

But despite its success, throughout my time at Brunel I always felt that the authorities looked down on boxing and did not regard it as a worthy and worthwhile pastime. Even later when I came back as the 1997 English amateur champion, you would think I had done nothing more than pass my driving test. I didn't expect to be mobbed on my return and I'm not someone who constantly needs to be told he's brilliant, but the odd nod in my direction or slap on the back would have been nice. As far as I could work out, boxing was just not something that nice college kids did. Allowances would always be made for the rugby, football and hockey boys: they would be given extensions for their essays and permission to miss tutorials and so on, even for regulation matches against other universities. But I was always being taken to task, even though I was pursuing my sport first at a national level and then on the international stage. Brunel, like most universities, is a predominantly middle-class institution while boxing is considered to be something from the street. The Marquess of Queensberry may have been the founding father of modern boxing and most public schools used to box, but times have changed and the sport has become an almost exclusively working-class pursuit, despite the interest it holds for the whole of society.

At first my tutors probably thought I was using boxing as an excuse to dodge my studies, but eventually I got the governing body (ABA) and later the Olympic Association to write letters explaining what was happening. I certainly found it tough to combine the two, especially in the countdown to the Commonwealths, which fell in the middle of the autumn term. I began to fall a long way behind in some areas of my studies and the quality of my work became erratic. In the end, it seemed sensible to take another year so that I could pursue my boxing ambitions and still come away with a degree. Although boxing began to take precedence over studying, I was determined to graduate from university, not least because I wanted some kind of safety net for later in life if, for instance, I was forced to retire from the ring early.

When my hernia problems were over and I returned to boxing in 1997, I was like an angry dog let off his leash. It had been a deeply frustrating year as I sat on the sidelines watching time flow by, taking the rest of the boxing world with it. I could do nothing about it as I watched my career fall further and further behind. The Commonwealth Games remained my goal but each day spent idle was a day wasted, an extra bit of experience lost. As a late-comer to boxing, I found time a more pressing factor than other boxers did.

This was both good and bad. It was bad in the sense that I had little time to waste. If I didn't make the Commonwealth Games in 1998, I almost certainly wouldn't make them four years later when I would be thirty-one. By that age I wanted to be on the professional circuit. But the urgency was also a good thing because it made me focus intensely. At the back of younger boxers' minds is the reassuring knowledge that, if they don't make one Games, they will probably have another chance two or four years later. That comfort zone didn't exist for me. If I screwed up now, that was probably my career over.

Life as a journeyman pro and sparring partner was probably my best and most realistic hope if I didn't achieve something significant at amateur level. And a mediocre career at amateur level would almost certainly lead to a mediocre career on the professional circuit.

But I had no intention of becoming someone else's punch bag and, if my enforced lay-off had any benefit at all, it was that it provided me with plenty of time to reflect on the past and focus on my future. Deprived of the thrill and adrenalin of competitive action, I began to brood about my misfortune. As the days passed, my frustration began to simmer, and by the time I stepped back into the ring in the yellow and green colours of Repton I was positively boiling. I felt like an unstoppable force and, without putting it too finely, anyone who stood in my way was going to get lamped.

While I was away from boxing I had had a recurring daydream about stepping on to the podium at the Commonwealth Games and stooping down for the gold medal to be placed around my neck. Nor was it just an exercise in the visualisation techniques I had learned. It was entirely spontaneous and natural and developed into something of an obsession. The image, in every detail, was the same each time: wearing a white tracksuit, one step on to the podium, I raise my arms aloft and do a 360-degree turn, acknowledging an ecstatic crowd as the camera homes in on my face. My emotions start to well up as I see my brothers in the crowd. I bend down and a gorgeous Malaysian girl with a lovely smile places the chunky gold coin over my head – I have dyed my hair gold for the ceremony. Then I stand tall, puff out my chest and the sound system booms out the National Anthem. I think about the rest of my family and mates back in north-west London, and all the people who had cast doubt on my ability to make it, sitting at home. I don't cry, but people can see I am choked by the whole experience.

Thinking about it now, several years on, I suppose there is nothing remotely original or remarkable about having a dream like this if you are a boxer or a sportsman – or anyone else with a burning ambition, for that matter. But it was significant at the time because it was very vivid and exactly the same in every detail each time I imagined it. The vision of myself definitely helped me get through that year. Without dreams there can be no hope, and without that hope to sustain me I might just have surrendered to circumstance and drifted away from boxing. I was just a plasterer waiting to happen.

On my return to the ring I stormed through to the ABA national semi-finals, having taken the London title. I knew I had to win the national title to get to the Commonwealth Games. Everything was going to plan, but in that fight for a place in the final I was knocked down for the only time in my career. My opponent was a bloke called Gavin McGhin from Sunderland, who caught me off guard and sent me arse first to the canvas. I had come out with my hands down and he hit me with a rapid combination in the first three seconds. I was more embarrassed than hurt, and a little surprised, because I had been brimming with confidence going into the fight. But I was feeling a bit fazed when I stepped into the ring following a last-minute row over the bandaging on my hand, which upset and annoyed me.

I had injured my knuckle at the start of the season in the first round of the ABAs against a guy called Mark Potter, who is a pro now. I won the fight by cutting him under his left eye, but I damaged myself when I caught him on the head with my knuckle. This was the injury that would dog my career for the next two years, causing me so much trouble in Sydney that I nearly had to pull out of the Games. I had fought through the ABAs carrying this injury, which had grown more and more painful with each fight and training session. I had been given a special type of bandaging to protect the injury, but just before the semi-final I was standing in the locker room all ready to walk out for the fight when the match adjudicator came in and ordered me to take off the bandaging and do it the orthodox way.

There had been another guy in the room who was a heavyweight from Sunderland. Just before the fight this guy slipped out of the room and told the adjudicator that my bandaging was suspicious. It did look a bit different but there was nothing wrong with it and the result was I was distracted at just the worst moment. So there was suddenly this great commotion in my room and all the officials were telling me to hurry up and get out there because the fight was about to start. I got bandaged up as quickly as possible and virtually ran out to the ring, leaving my concentration and my game plan back in the locker room in all the confusion.

Within a minute I was sitting on the canvas rubbing my chin and looking up at this bloke from Sunderland after he had landed a big one on me. He just came out of his corner swinging like a pub brawler and caught me unawares. I had quite a relaxed style in those days and should have had my gloves up higher to protect my face better. I had never seen the canvas from such close quarters, and once again I had this sinking feeling that my best-laid plans were in danger of being torpedoed. But I picked myself up and, although it took me a while to recover my poise, I bit hard on my gum shield and slowly boxed my way back into the fight, picking him off slowly and methodically. By the final bell I had edged him 11–8 to reach the final, and a great sense of relief flooded through me. There was no joy in the victory, just a sense of having got out of jail. It was a close shave and, although I had boxed like a clown and should have hammered this guy, I was pleased that I had shown the resilience to battle to victory. A couple of years earlier I might have not have had the ability to do that.

I had reached the final in my first year back and I was now

just one fight – about ten minutes away – from the 1997 national title. It was against a guy called Nick Kendall from Torquay and was shown on BBC *Sportsnight*, the first time I had ever been on television. I suppose the presence of the cameras and a big crowd should have made me more nervous than normal, but I was buzzing that night. I was so close to realising the first stage of my dream that I wasn't going to let the moment be stolen by anxiety. I was lifted by the whole experience and the guy never had a chance. I knocked him out in the first round. It was my fourth attempt to win the national title, and I had finally done it.

You can't do any more as an amateur than win the national title, but to my amazement and annoyance I still wasn't given an England vest. Some people said I should just forget about the Commonwealth Games and the Olympics three years later, and advised me to turn professional. But I knew I was just a novice and still had a hell of a lot to learn, so I decided to stick it out for another year on the ABAs. I just refused to go away until the authorities were forced to accept that I was the best amateur super-heavyweight in the country. If I won the national title for a second year running I figured they would have no choice but to pick me, while at the same time I would be proving my commitment to fighting for England. It was a gamble that paid off, as I reached the final again without any serious trouble. I was up against a guy, from Birmingham called Dean Redmond, a chubby guy but he could box a bit. This year the final was shown on Sky Sports but the result was the same. I destroyed him in the second round with a blitz of punching that left him sprawling on the canvas.

A week later I got the telephone call I had been waiting for. I had been picked for England. There was no time to celebrate, because as soon as I put the phone down I started packing my suitcase to join up with the England team for the Multi-Nations tournament in Venice. Our coach for that event was a guy called Terry Edwards, whom I was to get to know very well over the next couple of years.

When I first met Terry, I thought he was a diamond. He was a cartoon character London cabbie, full of attitude and wit, and I thought he could do no wrong. He was all mouth and made you feel like his best mate from the moment you met him. I listened to everything he said (and he said a lot), and in those early days when I had a lot to learn the advice he gave was good. I really believe he had my interests at heart. He was from the old school of London boxing who believed in discipline and doing everything the 'right' way. He didn't allow any swearing, and anyone he trained had to look smart and behave with good manners. I thought this was great. He made me feel like I was part of a club.

In the first round of the Multi-Nations I beat a little French bloke, as wide as he was high, in a really tight fight, and then reached the semis by stopping a very experienced Hungarian. A lot of people said that as a novice I would be in trouble against this guy, but I boxed really well and the referee had to intervene because he was taking so much punishment.

This was my first international tournament since I took up boxing and I had no idea what to expect in terms of the quality of the opposition. Back in England, everyone on the amateur circuit knows most of his rivals in his division, or at least knows *of* them, and is aware of what he will be up against. But there is much less chance of coming up with a pre-arranged game plan in these international competitions, except when you face one of the bigger names, because you simply have no idea about their style or temperament. To some extent you are swinging in the dark unless one of your team has prior knowledge of the opponent or has caught one of his earlier-round fights. But after my victory over the highly fancied Hungarian my confidence began to swell, and in the semi-final I had little difficulty in beating my Greek opponent.

The victory not only secured me a place in the final on my international debut, it also ensured my qualification for the European Championship finals. The final, against a German boxer, turned out to be the easiest fight of my life. In fact, Mr Blobby could have beaten the guy – because he never showed up. I like to think that he had seen me box in earlier rounds and suddenly remembered he had an unmissable appointment with his dental hygienist back in Hamburg.

In all likelihood, the German had achieved all he wanted to at the tournament by qualifying for the European Championships and didn't want to risk registering a defeat on his record or, even worse, getting knocked out and given an automatic twenty-eight-day lay-off. I would like to have fought him to have removed any doubt that I was the true winner, but the gold medal felt special all the same. This victory represented a new level to me and, although the tournament was no tougher than the English ABAs, it gave me my first taste of international competition and lifted my confidence a few more notches. I had stepped into unknown territory against boxers I knew next to nothing about, forcing me to think on my feet, to work out their style quickly and come up with a game plan to beat them.

Mine was the last fight of the tournament, as the superheavyweight bouts always are at these meetings, and afterwards Terry, myself and the other two England representatives, as well as some of the boxers from other countries, headed into Venice to celebrate. Chris Bessey had also won gold, as a light middleweight, so everyone in the party was in high spirits at the end. My working relationship with Terry had got off to the perfect start and we seemed to think the world of each other. There we were in one of the most beautiful cities in the world with an international gold medal safely in my pocket and the prospect of even greater achievements lying before me. We had a party that night and, as we stood in a bar by the canals in Venice, raising our glasses to our victories, little could I have imagined that my association with Terry would take such a sharp downturn and end amid such controversy behind the scenes at the Olympics two years later.

That tournament was in March and two months later, after a couple of England training camps at Crystal Palace, we set off to Minsk, the capital of Belarus in the former Soviet Union, for the European Championships. After my performance in Venice I was feeling very optimistic about my chances, but disaster struck the night before I was due to leave and the tournament turned into a nightmare for me. My brother Terry and I were moving flats from the top floor flat to the ground, and we were trying to shift everything as quickly as we could so I could get ready. In the rush our tempers began to fray, we started arguing badly, and in the rumpus I cut my hand on some glass and had to go straight to Accident and Emergency at Northwood Park Hospital where I sat for four hours in the early hours of Saturday morning.

When the doctors finally saw me, they said they couldn't stitch it because the wound would probably open again when I boxed and so they sprayed it with this skin-like glue. As injuries go, these are the worst for boxers. If you strain a muscle in your leg or cut yourself anywhere except your head or hands, you might be able to carry the injury so long as it isn't too serious – but your hands are obviously your main tools. Unfortunately the glue didn't really hold and my injury continued to bleed heavily. There are so many nerve ends in your hands and fingers that cuts are always that much more painful there. If you have ever had just a tiny paper cut, you will understand the grief my throbbing hand was giving me.

I was very depressed on the plane on the way out there. I had only recently earned the England vest I so desperately craved, I was heading to the European Championships to face some of the best amateur fighters in the world in my biggest-

Educating Audley... in my gown and mortarboard after graduating from
Brunel University.

**Above** With the boys from the boxing club I ran at Brunel… I'm the little one at the back!
**Below** Standing tall… on the top podium after the Multi-Nations tournament in Liverpool.

**Above** Have some of that… Macaque hits the canvas as I clinch Commonwealth gold in 63 seconds.
**Below** Easy tiger… the taste of success in Kuala Lumpur.

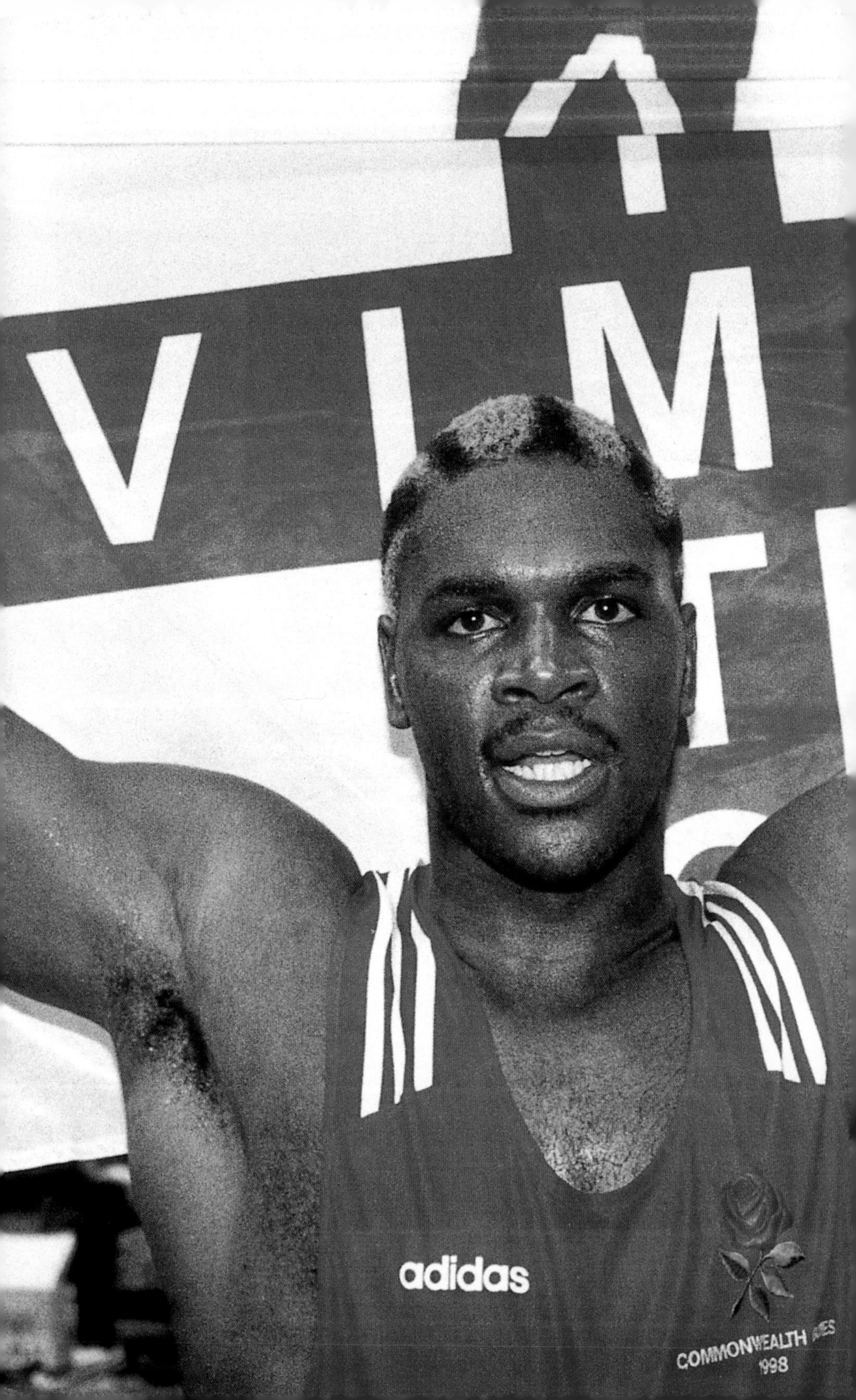

adidas
COMMONWEALTH
1998

**Inset** Being a boxer isn't all bad…
with the middle distance runner
Kelly Holmes during the
Commonwealth Games.

**Main** Acknowledging the crowd
after my Commonwealth glory.

**Above** With my friend and then Repton club-mate Courtney Fry at the Florida State University in preparation for the World Championships in Houston, Texas.

**Below** A break from training on the Gold Coast... Courtney (left) and myself with our sparring partners Harry Senior and Andrew Lowe (far right).

ever tournament, I had trained as hard as I ever had to get myself into top condition – and there I was crammed into my little seat clutching a cut hand after a stupid family ruck. My only hope was that, since the super-heavyweight bouts would, as usual, be the last fights on the programme, and as the tournament didn't start until Sunday, I would have the better part of two days for the cut to seal up. When we arrived at Minsk airport, we went straight to the hotel where the boxers had to register and when I checked the schedule for the tournament, I was a little taken aback. The super-heavyweight bouts were the first in the programme, to take place in about fourteen hours' time in the early afternoon. It was the first time in my experience of these tournaments, and that of the coaching team, that the card had been reversed, with the lightest divisions coming at the end of the programme and the heaviest at the beginning.

To make matters worse, I was drawn in the first round against the local favourite, Sergei Leyakhovic, the 1997 World Championship bronze medallist. When I stepped into the ring the next day I had no idea how my hand would hold up, because I hadn't dared test it on the punch bag in case I made it worse. So I started the fight against one of the pre-tournament favourites effectively with one hand tied behind my back in front of a seriously partisan crowd. I don't know much about Belarus as a country, but I guess they normally haven't got too much to shout about in the international sporting arena and so they were giving it everything during this fight. I often start fights slowly, as I try to size up my opposition and spot the flaws in his game and work out his general game plan, but on this occasion, with one hand bleeding in my glove and causing me real agony, I was really tentative in the first two rounds.

My strategy was based on defence and my plan was to try and dodge him hitting me and then catch him with a rapid counter-attack, either knocking him out or forcing a stoppage by cutting him around the eyes. (In amateur boxing, you score points based on the number of clean punches the judges see you land, and if there is no stoppage or knockout the winner is the one who has made the most connections. It's a bit like fencing, just more painful.) I just hung in there at the beginning and then started to open up as the adrenalin surging through me brought out my competitive instincts. Adrenalin is the best painkiller known to man: and in the heat of the fight my hand became less painful, and in the last three rounds I began boxing really well. After the fight, when I took my gloves off, my wound had reopened and when the adrenalin subsided it began to throb worse than it ever had.

The crowd were roaring on the local favourite, but they were also excited because they were watching a genuinely good fight. I caught my opponent with a stinging upper cut and for a moment I thought he was going to go down, but the bell was not long away and he made it through to the end of the round. I fought my way back into it, and when the final bell rang I felt I had done enough to edge it. I stood around nervously awaiting the verdict of the five judges.

It was a 5–5 draw. But in amateur boxing you can't have a draw so they do what's called a count-back. Normally, to score a point, three judges of the five who oversee a contest have to press their buttons within a second to register that a punch has been landed, but in a count-back they add up the points based on punches which all of the judges have pressed for and which do not count as points in the first system. The Belarussian was awarded the fight 25–21. When the score was announced, I was delighted to hear half the crowd boo and jeer. I wasn't the only one in the arena to think that I had got the better of him by the end. Even he raised my hand after the result was announced. The defeat was a blow, but it might have been immaterial anyway after I saw the state of my hand a few minutes later. It had opened up so badly that in all likelihood I would have had to withdraw from the competition. If there was any consolation to be drawn from this unhappy episode in Minsk, it was that I left knowing that I had come within a whisker of beating one of the best amateurs around with just one hand. And if there was a lesson to be drawn from the experience, it was don't move house with your brother the night before a major competition.

The big problem was that the Commonwealth Games were just four months away and, if I had done well in Minsk, I would have taken a major step towards making the England team and feeling confident about my chances out there. But time and tournaments for proving myself were running out. The next major event in the amateur calendar was the Multi-Nations in Liverpool in June. The competition was growing in status by the year and the quality of the boxers entering had been getting better and better, so I saw the event as my last big chance to stake my claim for the Commonwealth squad. The England camp told me that if I won in Liverpool my place was virtually assured and that, even if I just performed well, I might still make it. I had the feeling that the England authorities were now starting to believe in me. I had been training with them for several months and had got to know the set-up well, and they saw my dedication in the gym and realised that I was hungry for success. I also knew that, after my main rivals like Danny Williams had turned pro, there were no other super-heavyweights in England who could compete with me at this time. So despite the Minsk setback I was far from downhearted about my prospects for Kuala Lumpur, and went to Liverpool bursting with self-belief.

When I got there my heart sank a bit when I saw that the world number three and favourite for the Commonwealth title, a guy called Faii Falamoe from New Zealand, had entered the tournament. I had known there would be good boxers, but I wasn't expecting anyone of his calibre to be there. Fortunately, though, he was put on the other side of the draw, which was a relief and meant I still had the chance to progress and impress before I had to face him in the later stages. But all my anxieties and all the hype around him proved to be unfounded. While I cruised into the semi-finals without ever being seriously troubled, Falamoe was beaten by an unknown Canadian, Patrice L'Heureux, in his second fight. I watched that fight, and I have to say I wasn't at all impressed by either of them. The Canadian was big and strong, but that was about it. He had no technical skills to worry me. I sat there in the crowd smiling to myself in the knowledge that, so long as I didn't make any stupid mistakes, I was on the way to the final. Sure enough, the Canadian was out of his depth and I eased into the final where I stopped a German called Kay Ahrendt in the third round to take the gold and book my place on the flight to Kuala Lumpur.

Everything had gone to plan and I now had a shot at a major title. For three years this had been my goal, and I had achieved it. Ever since I learnt about the importance of setting myself one main goal and subordinating everything else in my career to realize it, I had thought of little else, in career terms, than getting to Kuala Lumpur. The next goal was the Commonwealth title, and I knew that if I could win it, an impressive achievement in itself, there would be no limit to the possibilities in my career. I would no longer have to prove my potential as a fighter. It might not have as much status as a world or Olympic title, but there are a lot of tough boxers in the Commonwealth. There would be much harder challenges ahead, but no one could ever say, 'He's just a journeyman who didn't quite have enough in the tank to go the whole distance.'

Making the Commonwealth team also brought a small but very welcome financial boost in the form of £700 per month grant from the National Lottery. Money, or the lack of it, was starting to become a major headache for me – my debts had climbed well past the £8000 mark and were rising by the month. When I wasn't pursuing my boxing career I was studying for my degree, and there simply wasn't any time left over to earn money. At the back of my mind I was always thinking – dreaming maybe – that one day, sooner rather than later, I would make the big time in boxing and would be able to clear my debts with one signature on a sponsor's cheque. But if this was ever going to happen, it was at least two years off, because I had always planned to try and get to the 2000 Olympics no matter what happened at the Commonwealths and no matter what offers I might receive to turn professional if I did well there.

My decision to go for gold in Sydney was a financial gamble with the highest stakes. I had no idea what the state of my bank account would be like by that stage, but it was fair to assume that I would be over £10,000 pounds in debt. And in boxing you are never more than a second away from a defeat that could knock you off your intended career path. I could be in the quarter-finals of the Commonwealths or the first round in the Olympics and pick up a cut on my eye that would end not only that fight but my part in the tournament.

In the ABAs there was always the following year to make amends, and it took me four goes before I was good enough to get it right and take the national title. But the Commonwealth and Olympic Games only come round every four years and you cannot afford to miss the opportunity for future success that they present. One of the saddest images I have ever seen in sport was the picture of the Italian 400-metre runner at the Los Angeles Olympics looking up in disbelief, his feet still in the blocks, after he had failed to hear the starting gun and all the other runners had sprinted off without him. Four years of preparation were wasted in that one second; four years of lying on his bed and dreaming of glory – or at least just competing – had come to nothing. Remember also the British runner Derek Redmond hobbling around the Barcelona track in tears and then being comforted by his Dad.

Their experiences sum up the risk of sudden failure or bad luck that haunts all sportsmen, but perhaps especially boxers. There is an element of snakes-and-ladders in all sports, but in boxing the ladders are a lot shorter and the snakes a lot longer. The margins for error are too fine. A punch from the blue, a small cut that won't stop bleeding, a pulled muscle in training – and your dream is over. Also, in boxing success is based on a chain principle: an early-round defeat or withdrawal from one major competition can cost you your appearance at the next. For instance – and this was what I was aware of as I prepared for the Commonwealths – if I slipped and got caught out by a stray haymaker from the bloke from Bermuda in the first round, I would return to England as a loser and my chances of making the Olympic team would be seriously undermined. If I was in the England hockey team, a similar mistake or accident might lead to a goal for the opposition but I – and my team-mates – would have the rest of the match and the other qualifying matches to make amends. In boxing there is no such comfort zone, no second chance. Nothing, I realised, could be left to chance, no preparation could be too thorough. If I screwed up in Kuala Lumpur, I might as well forget about Sydney.

The lottery funding we received was a great help in the countdown to the Commonwealth Games. Kuala Lumpur was going to be hot and humid and the conditions were almost certainly going to influence what happened in the ring, especially for those who had been brought up in cool climates like England, where the official season ended in May in any case. You only have to watch the television footage of Ulsterman Barry McGuigan struggling in 129-degree heat in his outdoor fight against the Texan Steve Cruz in Las Vegas in 1986 to realise the importance of conditions. McGuigan fought like a hero and your heart goes out to him when you see him almost dying in his boots – in the end it was the heat, not Cruz, that cost him his world title. With experiences like that in mind, we decided to invest some of the lottery money on some warm weather conditioning and headed to Tallahassee in Florida for three weeks of steamy sunshine, intensive training and, as it turned out, a few tasty rows before travelling to Malaysia.

# CHAPTER 5
# GOLD RUSH IN THE EAST

B efore flying out to Florida we began the countdown to the Commonwealths in the unlikely setting of the cathedral city of Chichester, a few miles from the south coast. It was there that the first rumblings of discontent among the England squad could be heard.

England had received a special World Class Performance grant from the National Lottery, which gave each boxer about £6,000 for subsistence as well as general funds for specific training programmes. Without that money half the team wouldn't have been able to go to Malaysia. One of the conditions was that a certain amount of the hand-out had to be spent on sports science. The England exercise physiologist, Marcus Smith had converted a room in the university to mimic the humid conditions of Malaysia. In theory it seemed like a good idea, but in practice the floor in the steam room, where the exercises took place was very slippery from all the condensation, which made it virtually impossible for us to shadow box and simulate proper fight conditions. Therefore the results were never going to be an accurate prediction of how our bodies would react once we were in Malaysia.

After a while the team realised that what we were doing

wasn't going to be much help and a few of the boys started sniggering.

I openly questioned the value of what we were doing and became a bit uncooperative, which caused some tension. It was like being back at school again: I was cast in the role of naughty pupil always causing trouble, always challenging authority. Yet I didn't care if I got people's backs up, because I thought it was important to demand why we were wasting time on a system which I thought was of no obvious advantage to any of us. But the answer was basically: 'Shut up, Harrison, just do it. We'll tell you what's good for you. You do your stuff in the ring and we'll tell you what you'll be doing outside of it.'

I believed I could see through this programme from the first few hours of being there. It seemed to me we were merely fulfilling a bureaucratic obligation laid down as a condition for getting the lottery funding. Here's some cash, now go and slide around on a floor in a steamy room in Chichester. I'm glad our prospective opponents at the Commonwealths couldn't have seen us: they would have been rolling around the floor in hysterics.

We also had to undergo a psychology programme which, again, on paper I had no problem with at all. I think psychology can play an important role in enhancing an athlete's role, so long as it is done properly. But there is good psychology and there is bad psychology. What works for one doesn't necessarily work for another and I knew from my studies that psychology was all about working with the individual. To me the programme seemed badly thought out, and I told the England management exactly what I thought of it. The psychologist assigned to us would come to each of the boxers in turn. He would ask us questions, we would answer them and then he would report back to Ian Irwin. There was no feedback to us at all, no advice from the psychologist about the practical applications of his findings. When we were asked to fill out questionnaires about mood and performance profiles, I lost my rag.

It seemed to me that once again, we were being asked to jump through a few bureaucratic hoops in order to fulfil the National Lottery criteria laid down by some pen-pushers. But we weren't allowed to question what we were doing. For me this was just more evidence of amateur athletes having to subordinate themselves to the authorities. If a man in a tie and blazer says jump, you are meant to jump. But I have never jumped for anyone unless I could see some real benefit for me. I wasn't going to get involved in what I saw as some *Carry On* farce just to keep these guys happy.

It was around this time that I had begun to implement for my own use the specific methodology and psychological profiling which I had tried out on my boxers at Brunel. I found these programmes very beneficial not just for me but also for other athletes and at the Commonwealth Games I became the England squad's unofficial psychologist.

By the time we left Chichester that day, all I had done was fill in some forms, have a one-way conversation with a psychologist and slide around in a steamy room wired up to some kind of Heath Robinson contraption. If Chichester had been mildly irritating and a taste of things to come, Tallahassee was a full blown, five-course feast of frustration laid on by the officials of the amateur boxing authorities. The team manager was a man called Brian Pollard, who made us hand over our passports as soon as we were through passport control so that we were virtually imprisoned in our training camp for three weeks. In the States you need to keep ID on you everywhere you go.

I found Pollard's attitude patronising, disrespectful, insulting and counter-productive and told him so. All of us in the England team were adults, some with families and jobs. Did the management team really think that, if it wasn't for them, we would go haring into the local bars on a week-long drinking binge? Did they not think we had sufficient sense of responsibility to decide for ourselves what was good for us? Did they really think that we would jeopardise our chances of Commonwealth gold, humiliate ourselves in the ring and undermine our career chances by behaving like delinquent kiddies? The whole experience felt a bit like that film *The Dirty Dozen*, with Brian Pollard as Lee Marvin putting together a team of twelve undisciplined hardened criminals who don't know what's good for them until he beats them into shape with a severe training regime that turns them into a formidable fighting machine to take on the might of the German Army. Give me a break.

All we wanted was the freedom to relax as we wanted, to see something of the town, maybe have a game of pool in a bar. It wasn't about going out and partying. We were in camp, and when you are in camp you are there to train – but we were also adults, and wanted to unwind as we saw fit. What we had was the choice of sitting around in our rooms twiddling our thumbs, or walking around like political refugees unable to behave like ordinary citizens. The whole experience reminded me of my prison days, with the boxers as inmates and the England management as the screws.

Once they took us on an official day out to a ranch owned by a local millionaire who laid on a fabulous barbecue for us. Everyone was really friendly and hospitable, but I felt annoyed by the way the management had decided that this was to be our 'fun day'. No one had asked us how *we* might like to spend our day off. They simply announced that the little boys were going to a barbecue. It felt like we were on parole and we were meant to be grateful to the management for their great generosity and fairness. We spent half a day there and I felt we were being paraded around like we were the management's pets at a provincial dog show. Once we had eaten and been shown off to the locals we just sat around waiting to get on our way while the management had their fun. That day out was a perfect illustration to me of the way the system seemed to work: management first, boxers second:

them joking around living it up, us sitting around bored out of our heads.

It was old school officialdom at its worst, a case of blazer knows best. Apart from anything else, I thought the management were in danger of making us miserable and undermining our squad morale. I vowed that when we got back from the Commonwealths I would kick up a stink and try to force the dinosaur establishment into a wholesale overhaul of their antiquated attitudes. It was the beginning of the clash with the amateur boxing authorities that would continue right up to my final fight in Sydney two years later. The most important people in the whole system were the boxers, but in the last few months, as we approached the biggest moment of our careers, we were treated with about as much respect as the kit bags we lugged around. The management seemed to think that they were our masters, not our servants. But as far as I'm concerned, they should have been responding to our demands and needs, not the other way around. And the manager is there to run the administrative side of a trip. He's not a headmaster, scout leader or prison governor.

Everyone else was frightened to speak up for themselves, so I became our unofficial spokesman and had several rows with Pollard before we flew out to Kuala Lumpur. Ian Irwin is a decent man who hates confrontation and he tried to act as mediator, but his main concern was that the boat didn't get rocked too heavily. He tried to appease both sides, but that approach rarely works. I felt sorry for him because he was the coach. His job was to train us, not act as a diplomatic go-between, but the fact that he had to get involved highlighted the fact that Pollard had succeeded in alienating the boxers. We had gone away a group of young sportsmen with their minds set on winning gold medals and doing themselves and their country proud, but felt we had been treated like naughty schoolboys.

The mood in Tallahassee was as bad as it could have been, but, ironically, the more the management tried to order us around, the closer we boxers bonded and the stronger we became as a group. Through no design of theirs, we forged a great sense of solidarity in the squad in those miserable few weeks in the heat of Florida before returning to England for a couple more training camps at Crystal Palace.

Not long before we flew out to Kuala Lumpur I saw an article in the *News of the World* highlighting the difference in financial status between Lennox Lewis and myself. It said Lennox was about to earn another £2 million from his fight against Croatian Zeljko Mavrovic in Connecticut to add to the £25 million he had already earned in his career. At that time in my life I had no car, I was in arrears on my rent, my debts totalled over £12,000 and I had no sponsor. Two of the hardest-up groups of people in Britain are students and athletes. I was both. Each day I was lugging my training bags on trains to and from the gym in Repton. Lennox, the article said, has a £1.5 million mansion in Hertfordshire, a Ferrari, an Aston Martin, a Range Rover and a plot of land in Jamaica ready for developing as a luxury retreat.

It was a timely reminder of the vast gulf that separates the top pro earners and those struggling to establish themselves in the amateur ranks of boxing. But it also acted as a spur. Lennox's career took off after he won gold for Canada at the 1986 Commonwealth Games and then at the Seoul Olympics two years later. Olympic gold was my dream too, but for the time being it had to remain a distant one: not a pipe dream, but one to be contemplated after the hurdle of the Commonwealths had been cleared.

My career was hanging by a financial thread at this time. It was only with the generosity of Repton, who raised £800 for me, that I had been able to get to the Multi-Nations that year, where I secured my place in the team. Repton were brilliant for me at this time – as was my now ex-girlfriend Hazel, whose accounting expertise helped me to balance the books and stave off bankruptcy. To some extent, though, the struggle has acted as a motivational force, focusing my attention more and more on the importance of not slipping at any stage or in any area of my preparations. As the stakes rose, so too did my urge for success. The struggle put fire in my belly.

There are four important areas of preparation for a boxer: physical, tactical, technical and mental. The England camp was very good at the physical side. You trained very hard, and all the English boxers were super-fit. Train, train, train. But that was about it. Technically, I learned virtually nothing on England camps. The pad work I did with Ian and Terry never changed. I found the training repetitive and the advice given to the boxers was little different whether they were a flyweight or a super-heavyweight. The technical challenges of boxing are different from weight to weight. You don't need to be a rocket scientist to understand that an 18-stone man moves in the ring a different way from a guy less than half his size. In the England camp Kelvin Travis was the person I found gave me the individual advice I needed on how to work on my style. You need feedback as a boxer, someone outside of the ring picking up on your areas of technical weakness. You might be developing a tendency to lower your gloves, or your stance might be wrong, but it is often difficult to notice these problems yourself and you need someone else's objective eye to spot them. I didn't feel the England camp in general used its imagination to tailor systems relevant to each individual.

Kelvin was the one trainer in the England camp I had a lot of time for. He was a tough guy from Manchester who gave the impression he didn't give a shit. He really did care about bringing on the boxers, and it was just his manner that made you wonder about him at first. He had a bit of a swagger and was always swearing and giving people a piece of his mind, but he was always on the side of the boxers, not the management, and I liked his rebellious, anti-establishment streak which reminded me of my club coach, Tony Burns. He wasn't just reading out of a textbook or toeing the official line. We had our moments and the sparks would fly occasionally, but I could relate to him. As a London geezer with jewellery and attitude, I was probably not the type he would necessarily take to, but there was mutual respect and we both gave as good as we got. I actually learned new ideas from Kelvin because he was willing to experiment with different approaches and explore my talents to see what else I had in my locker.

Despite the frustrations and rows that had marred our build-up to the Commonwealth Games, I still felt very confident about my chances of winning gold. You never know what you might find yourself up against at a big tournament like this with guys coming from all over the world, but my biggest threat was supposed to be Falamoe, the powerful New Zealand Maori. But after I had seen him getting beaten by a pretty ordinary opponent at the Multi-Nations I knew that I was a better boxer and that, provided I didn't do anything stupid, I would beat him if he we met.

I had to win gold in Kuala Lumpur. Bronze or silver would have been no good and I went on record to say as much. This was my chance to make a splash, to emerge from the relative anonymity of the ABA world and hold up my medal to show that I had the potential to make an impact at the highest level. The Games were being televised on terrestrial television and all the British papers, the international news agencies and radio stations would be out there. Promoters would also be there, hanging around at the ringside to spot the new talent coming through. Kuala Lumpur was not just a chance to win some glory for my country and for myself, it was also a shop window, a showcase event where I had the chance to raise my profile and catch the right people's eye. At the time I flew out to the Far East no one thought I had a chance of winning gold – maybe a bronze if I was lucky. The consensus amongst the 'experts' in the boxing world seemed to be that I had not done enough in the past to make gold a realistic possibility, and those setbacks early in my amateur career were supposed to be the proof. Only I knew it was possible. There were guys with better records than me heading to Kuala Lumpur, but no one with a greater urge to succeed.

Before flying out, I organised a party for the England boxing team at the Emporium in the West End, partly as a send-off but also to raise a bit of cash for each fighter. (The ABA had failed to organise anything themselves.) I advertised it as a rave and about 500 people turned up, raising about £1,400 for the squad.

The 1998 Games were the biggest in the history of the event since they began in 1911 as a 'Festival of Empire', where competitors from Britain, Australia, Canada and South Africa competed in track and field, boxing, wrestling and swimming. (It wasn't until 1930 that the Games began in earnest.) In 1998, the programme included everything from lawn bowls to cricket and rugby union. The six thousand athletes, back-up staff and officials from sixty-eight countries were housed in a giant village with purpose-built apartment blocks, shops, training facilities and a giant dining hall capable of seating up to two thousand people at once. I had never been to an event of this scale and had no idea about what to expect, but the general facilities in Kuala Lumpur were pretty good. I shared an apartment with four others, who were in two double rooms while I had the single to myself. (Who was going to argue?) Courtney Fry, the light heavyweight, was probably the guy I knew best before flying out because we both boxed at Repton together.

We had a few minor problems, like no towels in our rooms and the toilet kept blocking (I'm sure it was Courtney). All these day-to-day details were Brian Pollard's responsibility as team manager, but he never did anything about them. We didn't expect Pollard to get down on his knees and sort the toilet out himself (although by the end of the trip I wouldn't have minded putting him in there head first), but he should have been the one chasing up the plumber. We wanted to concentrate on what we were there for: to box. But because Pollard wasn't sorting out the daily admin for us, we ended up doing these things ourselves. We had to go out and collect and return our own towels. We had to chase up the camp officials to get the toilet unblocked. When you are representing your country you don't expect to spend half a day trying to find a local plumber or searching for a clean towel or a launderette.

The morale amongst the boxers was generally good. All the back-up staff were great: the physios, the doctors, the officials and even the trainers, Ian Irwin, Terry Edwards and Kelvin Travis were really helpful. We all got on well, and the team pulled closer and closer together as the tournament progressed. The only fly in the ointment was Pollard, but we weren't going to let him ruin the biggest event of our lives.

I loved every minute of life on the camp. By the end of the Games, I had spoken to every person in the England team. I was Mr Communicator and went around entertaining the troops to boost morale: winding people up, pulling pranks, holding court in the cafeteria, singing rap and soul songs. I was England's self-appointed unofficial court jester for the Games, and it wasn't long before everyone in the camp knew who I was. (You could hardly miss me even if you wanted to. I had dyed my hair with gold streaks, tiger-style.)

All the British teams, as well as those of many of the other nations, would end up eating together in the main hall, and at first the English boxers would sit with the English boxers, the Welsh athletes with the Welsh athletes, the Scottish swimmers with the Scottish swimmers and so on. Everyone stayed with the gang they knew, but I started parking myself down with the gymnasts, the weightlifters or the athletes. Each time I would sit somewhere different and I like to think that in a small way my antics helped to bond the team, creating a sense of unity and an air of relaxed confidence amongst the Brits. After a few days, you could notice the mood in the camp rising and there was a really happy feel to the place. I'm not saying that it was all down to me, but I'm sure my pratting around and general aura of unembarrassed self-confidence rubbed off on a lot of people. If you chuck a few hundred strangers into a camp together there is bound to be a bit of reserve and uneasiness at first, but I thought it was important from a performance point of view to gee everyone up, instil a sense of exuberance into the place. You don't want to go into your competition feeling tense. Having a few nerves is only natural and good, but if you are tense and don't have good feelings about your environment or the people round about, you are not going to perform to the best of your abilities. Apart from anything else, there we all were, the best athletes in the country in our field, and this was going to be one of the high spots of our careers and lives. How many other people would be able to say they had performed for England at the Commonwealth Games? This was one of those rare chances of a lifetime, which you have to seize and then wring every drop of enjoyment and satisfaction from it.

The way the draw worked out meant that it was going to be several days before I would have my first fight – against the favourite, Falamoe. No one thought I could beat this guy, and the other athletes seemed to think that I was going to have just the one fight and that was the reason why I appeared so carefree around the village. They thought I was just here for a laugh, living it up while I could. But in fact it was exactly the opposite. I was relaxed and full of myself because I knew I could beat Falamoe and win the gold.

The Shah Alam Stadium, where the boxing was staged, was a total disappointment. Most of the other venues were tightly packed together so that spectators could get to the main area and move from one venue to the next with relative ease. But for some reason they put the boxing out in the middle of nowhere, about forty-five minutes away from the other venues and with poor transport, so most of the other athletes didn't make the journey down until the finals. The response from the Malaysian public was also disappointing, because there weren't many of their guys who stood much of a chance. So most of the time we were fighting in a largely empty venue and could hear individual voices echoing around the giant arena. To come to a big event like the Commonwealths and fight in such an atmosphere was depressing, to say the least. You get a better atmosphere in Merthyr Tydfil or Preston. But there were about a hundred core English supporters made up of family, friends and coaches from back home, and they did their best to create some noise.

I had just three fights to win Commonwealth gold. For the first, against Falamoe, there were probably no more than a thousand spectators present – which would have been fine if the capacity of the stadium was a thousand, but there was room for at least five times that and so it looked and sounded dreadful. It was not quite how I had imagined the launch of my medal dream when I was lying on my bed back home in London.

My performance was a little flat, but I had the fight under control and always felt that I had enough in the tank to pull away if he started closing on me. There was nothing particularly interesting about the fight itself, and it was not one that would stay in the memory for long, but mentally it gave me a great boost. I beat him by 11 points to 8, and I could see no one else left in the field with the ability to stop me taking the gold. The victory, against a lot of people's favourite for the title, attracted a reasonable amount of press attention at the time, but ensured a lot more in the semi-finals. At that stage of the Games, there are only so many events the papers can cover. There is no way they can have a reporter at every single sport, so most of the papers rely on the agencies for copy.

I had secured myself a bronze medal by reaching the semis,

where I was going to face the winner of the fight between the Canadian Patrice L'Heureux and Australian Justin Whitehead. On the day of their fight I decided to head into the venue to check out my prospective opponent as well as lend my support to the other England boys. The transport to and from the village to the venues was probably the worst aspect of the facilities. The buses were infrequent and unreliable, and standing around at a bus stop or sitting on a stationary bus is not really what you want when you are gearing up for the most important event in your career.

On this occasion we had been sitting around for about forty-five minutes with the driver just reading the paper. It was a boiling hot day and everyone was getting fidgety and started moaning and mopping their brows. I was getting more and more frustrated, and eventually I completely lost my temper with the driver. I stormed up to the front of the bus and started shouting at him to get moving. When the handrail I was gripping broke off in my hand, the driver turned on the engine and said, 'OK, boss, we go venue.' When I turned round I saw the Canadian guy L'Heureux a few seats away, looking at me with wide staring eyes like I was some kind of lunatic. I could see what he was thinking: 'Jeez, that's the beast I'll be fighting in the next round if I get through.' It was a perfect opportunity to gain some kind of psychological advantage, so I glared at him through my wraparound shades and he quickly looked down at his feet before I walked slowly to the back of the bus. The Canadian lost his fight a few hours later, but even if he had got through I knew I had beaten him already.

I don't know why, but I wasn't feeling quite right when my fight against Whitehead got underway. It was just one of those bad days. I was doing enough to keep my nose in front and was just beating him up slowly. As I sat down in the corner at the end of the second round, Terry Edwards said, 'Come on, Audley, you're making a young man feel very, very old. Get your shit together.' And then he slapped me around my head. Some boxers don't mind getting smacked about by their coaches, but I do. No one had ever done that to me before. I was so incensed that I jumped off my stool at the bell and within seconds I had landed a massive cross on Whitehead, who went down like a rag doll. That was it. The fight was stopped. I had won and I was into the final. When I punched the guy I was thinking of Terry Edwards. I still don't like what he did, because I don't think it was a trick intended to snap me out of my lethargy – I think he was just taking liberties. But, intentional or not, it certainly got my blood up and brought the fight to a rapid conclusion.

The gold medal was now within my grasp. The final, against Michael Macaque of Mauritius, was the last event of the tournament. The crowd was the best it had been for the whole tournament, mainly because it was the finals but also because a Malaysian guy had made it to his final and, although half of the crowd disappeared straight afterwards, there was still a great atmosphere. There were also about forty guys from the press, plus the television crews and a few radio people. It was, by some distance, the biggest press contingent to sit ringside at one of my fights. This was my big moment, the one I had been waiting for four years, and Tony Burns, my coach from Repton, was also there with about four others from the gym. If I lost, it would be a big setback for my ambitions – because I would still need to convince people that I was a major force to be reckoned with. Win – and the dream was one step closer to becoming a reality.

Before the fight I was lying on the couch in the changing rooms feeling sorry for myself, with my foot and hand both wrapped in ice. The stress fracture in my foot had flared up and was giving me grief, and my hand was just as painful. I had had an operation on it before the Games, but the pain and the swelling had erupted again. I was throbbing with aches and my pre-match adrenalin was starting to flow. The biggest moment of my career was just thirty minutes away, a vital stepping-stone in the career path I had laid out for myself. Now I sat there thinking that I might be forced to withdraw because of my injuries.

There were two doctors in my room, a physio, Terry, Ian and Kelvin as well as a handful of officials and other boxers. I was starting to feel claustrophobic, crowded out by all the people who were coming in and out like my changing room was the local post office. Finally I snapped and got up, flailed my arms around, kicked a bucket against the wall on the other side of the room and started shouting: 'Get out, get out, get out! I'm ready – take that ice off my hand and foot.' Nobody hung around for long. I had just about calmed down and got myself into a controlled and focused state when my peace of mind was shattered again. I still don't know whether there was anything behind what happened next, and for a while I thought I was going to be disqualified. There are some very dubious goings-on behind the scenes in amateur boxing and nothing would ever surprise me.

In amateur tournaments you are not allowed to pick your own gloves like you can in professional boxing. Just before I was due to walk out for the fight the officials came into my changing room and handed me two pairs to choose from. I didn't like the feel of either of them, but one pair was much worse than the other and was really constricting, bringing on the pain in my knuckles when I hit the pads. After I had put on the other pair the officials disappeared, and I had a few minutes to myself psyching up and shadow boxing. I was right in the zone, fully focused on fighting this guy, as I walked out of the changing room towards the arena. But as I headed down into the arena all these officials from the International Amateur Boxing Association (IABA) descended on me in a frenzy, shouting: 'You can't wear those gloves – they're the wrong ones!

Harrison, stop! Harrison, you are not fighting with those gloves on.'

They had told me to wear a particular set of gloves, so I did, but here they were five minutes later telling me to take them off. I was with the coach, Ian, and I felt he should have stepped in and read them the riot act, but I think he was just as stunned as I was by what was happening. So there I was moments before the most significant few minutes of my career, arguing with officials, shaking my head in disbelief. I put on another set of gloves – by a different manufacturer which, ironically, were a hell of a lot better than the ones I had just taken off. Ian asked me if I wanted more time to warm up, but I was so angry I said he must be joking and I bounced into the arena and into the ring like a bull after the picadors had finished with him.

Far from distracting me, the fiasco with the gloves had the opposite effect. I was positively raging, and my opponent never stood a chance with me in this frame of mind. Normally I like to start slowly, weighing up my opponent and wearing him down before stepping up the battering in the second half of the fight. But not on this occasion. The final lasted 63 seconds. I stalked the Mauritian around the ring, lined him up and floored him with a huge left cross which sent him crashing into the ropes. It was only the fourth punch I had thrown. He fell forward on his knees and there was no way he was going to be getting up for more. I was Commonwealth Games champion.

The medal ceremony took place almost immediately. It wasn't quite how I had imagined it in my dream: instead of a beautiful girl putting the medal around my neck, it was some middle-aged bloke in a blazer. Even so, I could barely contain my delight. After four years of mounting expectations, serious injuries, rows with the England authorities, occasional moments of doubt after a demoralising defeat, gruelling training regimes and rising debts, I had finally achieved what I had set out to do. This was the moment that I had visualised and here I was all those years later living it out for real.

Immediately after the final I grabbed an England flag – the cross of St George – and ran around the arena. I was surrounded by dozens of little Malaysian kids who came up to my waistband, and I handed them a wad of signed photographs that I had put into my kit bag before leaving the village. I have always been aware of marketing and PR opportunities, and I wasn't prepared to miss out during the most high-profile moment of my career. I wanted to prove myself as an athlete in the ring, but also to establish myself as a personality outside it. If there had been a baby in the crowd I would have kissed it. I'm better than Tony Blair when it comes to photo opportunities.

The BBC crew got all four of England's gold medallists together and I rapped another poem for the cameras. I had been doing this throughout the tournament every time I was in front of the cameras. Some of the songs were rehearsed, others spontaneous. I wanted to make a public exhibition of myself out in Kuala Lumpur, but it was a calculated gamble. I planned to do everything possible to make an impression while I had the exposure. It was calculated, because if I goofed and came back with a bronze or no medal at all I would have looked a bit of a clown, a mouthy show-off with ambitions beyond his abilities. But although it may have seemed that I was horsing around a lot, I was incredibly focused on the boxing. I couldn't afford to mess up and when I trained and fought there was nothing carefree about me. I was two different people in Kuala Lumpur: a happy-go-lucky show-off in front of the cameras, but behind the scenes whenever I taped up my hands and put on my gloves I was intense and focused.

I wasted no time in telling the world's press about my plans for the future: 'I'm going to win the Olympic crown, then I'm going to be professional heavyweight champion of the world. I have absolutely no doubt about my ability to keep these promises.' I remember some of the journalists looking at me sceptically, as if they were thinking, 'Yeah, right, Audley. Well done, lad, you've won the Commonwealth gold – but let's not get too excited, shall we?' But this wasn't just the adrenalin talking. I meant it. I didn't care if people said I just talked a good fight, because I was going to carry on showing them that I could fight a good fight too. I wanted my comments to find the back pages, to help build my profile and start some momentum for the Olympics. Winning the Commonwealths provided me with the platform from which I could announce myself to the British public loud and clear. The next day I got great press, just as I had hoped. I had given all the journalists their angle on the story and their headline: 'Harrison promises Sydney gold.'

That evening, I could properly let my hair down for the first time in months. I couldn't remember the last time I had had a drink, but after my victory I headed up with the other boxers to the beer garden at one end of the village to celebrate. I couldn't believe the reaction of everyone there, as I was swamped not just by the English and the other Brits but by the other athletes and officials from all the different countries. Maybe it was because my fight had been one of the last events and people had been tuning in to get a final glimpse of the Games they had been a part of. Maybe it was because I had been a bit of a personality around the village. Maybe it was because I had sung those impromptu raps. Or perhaps it was just that I had been going around telling everyone, 'I'm going to win gold. Just you watch.' And now I had.

Whatever it was, and I'm not being big-headed, everyone (especially the ladies) wanted a piece of me that night. I must have posed for about fifty photographs with other athletes. It was the first time in my life that I had experienced the adulation of strangers. It was a weird but exciting feeling seeing people glowing in my aura, treating me as if I was more special than them. When I used to lie awake at night imagining myself winning the Olympics or the world professional heavyweight title, I had no idea what it would be like to be famous. It was my first taste of fame, and I have to admit that I wasn't fazed by it at all.

But I wasn't the only Englishman with something to celebrate that night. Three others – Aldershot-based soldier and light middleweight Chris Bessey, middleweight John Pearce and my friend the light-heavy Courtney Fry – had all won golds too. Gary Jones, the light flyweight from Liverpool whom I was always being photographed with because he was 7 stone and I was 18, won a bronze, as did lightweight Andrew McLean. Half the team had won medals, and England were the top boxing nation at the Games.

Later that night, all the boxers and a few of the other athletes went into Kuala Lumpur to hit some bars and clubs. We had been warned about going into town because the political unrest, which had been sweeping the country during the Games, had led to more riots in the capital. We saw nothing and knew very little of what was going on in the streets during the Games, as were cocooned away in our village. We had been told that the rioting was pretty severe in some areas and that there were running battles between protesters and riot police, with Molotov cocktails being thrown and tear gas canisters fired. We decided it would be a good idea to avoid the flashpoints and headed out to the Hard Rock Café in a safe part of town. For want of a better expression, we had a riot. It was already probably the best day of my life. I had won a gold medal after four years of hard work and eight years after I had taken up boxing. My Olympic dream was alive, England were the top nation at the Games in my sport and I had made a bit of a name for myself back home. As we went from bar to bar and club to club, it didn't seem that my day could get any better.

But it did. Someone had caught my eye back in the village over the previous few weeks but I thought the opportunity would never present itself. She had the looks and the personality and she was the one woman at the Games I would have liked to become intimate with. I felt she was in a different league, completely untouchable, and I never had the balls to act on my passion. But it happened, and I honestly felt like I was floating. It was just passion, a passion that neither of us could contain any longer. It was completely surreal, like an out-of-body experience. I couldn't believe it was happening to me and I had to keep pinching myself and saying, 'Audley, this is really, really, happening to you. It's not a dream.' I'm not going to mention any names because she's a good friend and I respect this lady too much and would never want to compromise her. But all I will say is that, if I dreamed the perfect day, this was it and she was the icing on the cake.

If I scripted a fantasy version of that day, it wouldn't match the reality of what happened. It was too unbelievable. I won the Commonwealth gold, which no one said was possible. I was suddenly mobbed by the press and the other athletes. I was on course for glory in Sydney. With a night of passion to remember to top it all off. That evening was a one-off and will never happen again, but I will never, ever forget a moment of it.

# CHAPTER 6

# TAKING THE FIGHT TO THE STREETS

The England boxing team were in a state of euphoria when we took off from Kuala Lumpur airport, but we certainly came down to earth with a heavy bump when we got back. It had been England's best performance for twenty years in the Commonwealth ring. We had put boxing back on the map, thrusting it into the forefront of the TV and media coverage by the force of our performances. Yet there was a stony silence from the London ABA for several weeks after our return – not even a letter of congratulation or a phone call. When a letter from the London ABA finally flopped through my letterbox I was surprised to read that I had been suspended from all amateur competition forthwith. Welcome home, Audley, you are officially sacked. I stood there in utter disbelief. Was this a wind-up, or had the ABA really managed to sink to these new depths? Who needs enemies. . . ?

Brian Pollard had written to the London ABA saying I owed him £75 that he had supposedly subbed me when the England team had some cheap but good-quality team suits made up before the tournament had got underway. As far as

I was concerned, that money came out of the National Lottery pool, but the letter informed me that I could not box again until I had paid the money. It was not quite the hero's welcome I had been envisaging and goes to show how far the relationship between the boxers and the authorities had sunk. I refused to pay the money because it was not money I thought I owed, and in the end the people at Repton settled it and I got my licence back.

Pollard, too, was suspended by the ABA over some comments he made to the local press about the organisation. Given how I felt he'd managed the team in Tallahassee and Kuala Lumpur, I was not sympathetic and when he took the ABA to court and was reinstated, I didn't see it as good news. If the boxers, the most important people in the sport (supposedly), didn't get on with him, it didn't seem to make much sense to have him in the set-up.

I had won a Commonwealth gold medal and was widely considered to be Britain's best hope of a boxing gold at Sydney. It seemed to me that the ABA must have realised that I'd be tempted to turn pro but, as an organisation, they did nothing to keep me amateur. I was too rebellious and had ruffled too many blazers. They wanted boxers who said 'yes' to everything and never challenged their attitudes and policies. As far as I could understand from my dealings with them, they would rather have a boxer lying flat on his back in the first round, but who asked no questions outside the ring, than one who could bring glory to his sport and his country but kicked up a row if he didn't agree with the system.

It says something terrible about the state of British amateur boxing if the officials would rather have a team of losers than winners, just so long as its members stood to attention when barked at. My respect for the amateur boxing authorities in this country is virtually non-existent. As far as I am concerned the sooner they are swept out in a huge spring-clean of the sport the better it will be for the future of amateur boxing.

Despite our success in Malaysia, the sport was in dire straits behind the scenes. Not long after our return, we were horrified to hear that the ABA had had their application for £4.5 million of lottery funding rejected. This was a devastating blow for a sport already on its knees and begging for the smallest amount of support. It was no exaggeration to say that its very existence was under threat. The short-term implications of this news were obvious. Most of Britain's top amateurs were unemployed or they were students. Only a few had an income to enable them to pay their own way. Without any cash, the boxers who had performed so creditably in Kuala Lumpur, including myself, would almost certainly have to turn professional.

The £700 per month we had been receiving to assist our preparations for the Commonwealths had been a great help but it had now come to an end. The sport as a whole was in dire need of financial assistance. My own personal financial struggle to keep going as an amateur boxer motivated and emboldened me to take on the establishment in the name of all amateur boxers. Unless you feel the pain of something your-self, it is difficult to be sympathetic to a cause: you only hear people moaning about their lot and asking for more money. But for my colleagues and myself on the amateur circuit the pain was real and the struggle has been and remains a worthy one.

I could no longer sit by and watch my sport being slowly wrecked. I decided it was time for me to get political and take on the establishment. I vowed that I would not box again until the sport received funding from the National Lottery. The punch with which I laid out Macaque in the Commonwealths turned out to be the last I would throw for almost ten months.

I wanted a complete overhaul of the sport from the tie-and-blazer brigade at the top to the quality of provincial gyms at the bottom. I wanted changes to what I saw as the random and unfair way the England team was picked, which was at the whim of the coaches; I wanted more television coverage (TV exposure is a sport's oxygen); I wanted significant sponsorship deals which could genuinely make a difference to a boxer's career; and I wanted boxers represented on the board of the ABA and the British Olympic Association. In short, at this time, amateur boxing had very little by way of cash, representation or public exposure, as well as a poor infrastructure and virtually no hope for the future. Year after year, decade after decade, the sport had failed to advance. It says something about the administrators that it took one of the boxers they supposedly represent (i.e. me) to force through reforms and secure its financial future. The finances of the ABA were in such a dreadful state that a few months before the Commonwealths the England team was only able to participate in an international tournament after the professional promoter Frank Warren made a contribution from his own pocket.

To challenge the best in the world, boxers need good facilities, but even more importantly they need the time to improve their craft. Boxing is a technical discipline as much as it is an exercise in power and strength of character. To improve technically, a boxer needs to work on his game, and he also needs good trainers and amenities. Time is money and boxers need cash to live – not a great pot of the stuff, but enough to let them get on with developing their talent without having to worry about how they can support themselves. It is an extremely important issue, because in the past many aspiring young amateur sportsmen and women – not just boxers – have been forced to give up their dreams because they know they will be in for years of financial hardship.

When we won the six months of funding for the Commonwealths an interim plan was put in place, and we had every reason to be confident that a permanent or long-term funding deal to see us to the Olympics and beyond would be arranged soon after we got back. But I feared a major defection of amateurs to the professional code after the ABA's application was given a qualified rejection by the lottery board, which meant that unless it could be sorted out, there would be no lottery money for boxers.

Proper funding gives sportspeople a better chance of fulfilling their potential and realising their dreams. It was surely no coincidence that Britain's overall performance in Sydney, their best since the *Chariots of Fire* Paris Games in 1924, came a few years after funding from the National Lottery was granted to the country's aspiring Olympians. Imagine what Britain's sportsmen and women might achieve at the Athens and Beijing Olympics when the infrastructure of so many sports will have improved even further. But looking back at the country's success in Sydney, it is difficult also not to feel a great sense of regret about all the wasted opportunities and unfulfilled British talents that went before.

The lack of funding goes right to the heart of the issue, and partly explains why British boxing has trailed so far behind that of the United States and the countries of the former Soviet Union. Amateur boxing is the grass roots of the sport, and it is from the ranks of amateurs that the professionals emerge. It is a blindingly simple equation: if amateur boxing is poor, so too is the professional game. In financial terms, Britain has been a potential heavyweight fighting as a bantamweight, starved of the support it needs to survive and thrive.

After one of my fights during the Olympics a couple of years later I saw a report in the *Daily Telegraph* which said: 'For years Britain has been to amateur boxing what Equatorial Guinea has been to swimming' – a reference to Eric the Eel, the swimmer who took half a day to finish his race. But the reporter was right: British amateur boxing has been poor, in both senses of the word, for my entire lifetime. In the 1960s there were over a hundred thousand registered amateur boxers. Today there are nine thousand. The ABA championship was once one of the highlights of the British boxing calendar. Nowadays it is virtually an irrelevance to the outside world. It used to be broadcast on BBC at prime time, and the likes of John Conteh and Alan Minter were household names. Amateurs were once as famous as pros, but these days the national ABA champions can sit on the proverbial Clapham omnibus and no one will pay them a blind bit of attention.

My experience at Stoke Newington police station and the legal battle that followed taught me that you could challenge the establishment and win. You didn't just have to sit there and accept the system as set in stone, and I decided that I would carry our cause to the very doorstep of 10 Downing Street if I had to. I had nothing to lose by taking on the authorities. My relationship with them could not get any worse, and their attempt to suspend me was the final straw. My success in Kuala Lumpur had raised my profile in the media and provided me with the platform I needed to state our case to as wide an audience as possible.

From where I stood in those immediate few months after Kuala Lumpur, Britain would almost certainly not be sending any boxers to Sydney. What a humiliation for a country that likes to consider itself one of the most powerful boxing nations in the world. No boxers at the Olympics! 'Look out, the Brits are coming .. Er, hang on, actually, they're not. They're all at home watching it on telly.'

I got all England's leading boxers together and told them I was setting up a body to represent them, called the Amateur Boxing Union of England. All the current internationals signed up, and I charged just £1 per boxer to help pay for stationery, telephone calls, faxes and so on. But the enterprise ended up costing much more than the small amount raised from membership fees and I was forced to draw on my own resources to see it through. I worked around the clock to get the operation up and running. Hazel (by now my ex-girlfriend but we were still very close) and Julie, the girlfriend of David Walker, one of the boxers, kindly gave me some help with the administrative burden. I drew up a manifesto, sent out press releases and called a press conference. I also drafted a Notice of Intention document and sent it to the ABA, to Tony Banks, the then Sports Minister, to media organisations and to all the boxing gyms. We drew up a petition complaining about the treatment of amateur boxers compared to other Olympic athletes, and set out to get as many signatures as possible with a view to handing it in to Banks, who was said to be a fan of boxing and who I had spoken to at the Commonwealth Games.

My efforts were about as much appreciated at the ABA as a bucket of cold sick, and I found myself blocked at every angle. They thought I was getting too big for my boots and that I was not just usurping their role but also suggesting, by implication, that they had not been doing their jobs well enough down the years. I could live with that – for the simple reason that I do not think many of them had done enough for the cause. There are dozens of good, competent men in the boxing establishment, but you only needed to look at the infrastructure and the lack of achievements and to talk to any of the hundreds of amateur boxers who had been forced to give up their dreams to understand that there was something wrong with the way things were being run.

Within a few weeks we had two thousand signatures on the petition and I organised a march on Parliament to hand it in to Tony Banks. I planned to do so the day England were fighting the USA in an international being televised live by Sky Sports from the Hilton Hotel in Park Lane. All the other boxers who had signed the petition and joined my union were on the card. Some of these guys had a lot more to lose than me, and they were too frightened to pull out in case they lost their place in the national team.

On the day I, a couple of dozen amateur boxers not fighting in the international and about fifty other boxing people met up outside the SW1 night club in Victoria where I worked as a door supervisor for the start of the march. The press were there in force, including journalists from the national and local papers and a television crew from the *London Tonight* programme. I took the media corps into the club and gave them all a free drink before I stood up and read out the Notice of Intention document. I felt a huge sense of excitement as everyone applauded when I finished my speech and I realised that other people believed in our cause.

We had had some banners made up, and as we walked up to Parliament Square holding them, cabbies and other drivers beeped their horns in support and bemused tourists took pictures of us.

We were allowed into the forecourt of the Houses of Parliament, where we handed the petition to an official to take it to Banks. That night I went up to watch the international against the United States, and by then everyone involved in amateur boxing knew about the march and the threat of strike action. The camera kept panning in on me and I was approached by all the journalists to talk about the march and the reasons behind it. The next day all the stories in the press were about the march with barely a mention of the international, which was exactly what I had intended. We had turned the issue into news: our story was now up and running, with some momentum behind it, and it wasn't going to go away until some action was taken. This would be an issue that could embarrass a lot of people in the run-up to the Olympics: the ABA, the lottery board, the British Olympic movement and the government. But ultimately it would be the image of the country that would suffer the most if Britain proved unable to raise the cash to back even a handful of its brightest prospects for the biggest event in the history of organised sport. That was the media part of the struggle sorted out. Now we needed to work on the government and get boxing on the agenda in the corridors of power.

Within a couple of weeks Tony Banks had written back to me, thanking me for my letter and petition and saying how surprised he was to hear about the terrible state of amateur boxing and its bleak future following the rejection of the ABA's application for lottery money. He said he would look into it, but as the facts stood it sounded very unfair that boxers were the only group of Olympic athletes without any financial backing.

While waiting for Banks to take the issue further, my next step was to target the British Olympic Association. The BOA has an athletes' commission with representatives from every sport – except boxing. It was incredible to think that baseball, softball, canoeing and volleyball all had a voice in the Olympic movement but that boxing, one of the Olympics' oldest sports, had none. I started lobbying the BOA and, to their credit, they were quick to get in contact and invite me on to the committee. They wrote to the ABA and asked why they had not put forward a representative, suggesting to them that they would be happy to have me join the committee as I had shown political initiative in lobbying them. The ABA ducked the issue by saying it was up to the national squad to choose its own representative. So I went back to the boxers, who unanimously endorsed me as their spokesman, and I was voted on to the committee, which met quarterly to discuss the concerns and needs of the athletes. Within just a few weeks boxing finally had representation in the British Olympic movement. Again, I was left wondering what the ABA had been doing all these years. All I had to do to get on to the committee was write a letter to them and make a couple of telephone calls. The BOA were only too happy for the boxers to join the party. It was hardly one of the Twelve Labours of Hercules.

I wrote to the ABA requesting a meeting with the board but I was declined. I tried to attend one board meeting after another but each time I was blocked for one reason or another. Eventually, I got in contact with senior figures in the ABA, telling them I was doing an academic feature on the current state of amateur boxing. I told them their views would be invaluable, and they were only too happy to participate. But it was just a hoax to force a meeting with them and when we met up I immediately confronted them with all the issues I had wanted to raise.

So the battle to get funding for boxing was now being waged on three fronts: through the BOA, through the media and through Tony Banks. The application, or the reapplication in this case, had to come from the ABA as they were the governing body. All the time during this political saga I knew exactly what was going on inside the ABA meetings as I had a mole in the camp, one of the good guys, who gave me all the information about what was happening behind the scenes (something I will be eternally grateful for). I had access to or copies of all the relevant documentation including the ABA's original application for the World Class Performance Plan as it was called, which left a lot to be desired.

Sport England, who are responsible for distributing lottery funds to sporting bodies, wanted all the money to be account-able so that they could guarantee that it was being spent wisely. This was not an unreasonable demand, but the ABA had failed to make clear how they would be able to do this. What was needed was the formation of a separate company, similar to the one they have in athletics, so that the money could be ring-fenced and properly managed. Sport England also wanted the ABA to start raising funds through sponsorship, which they had failed to do in the past. Boxing was one of the few Olympic sports without an official sponsor to invest money in the development of new talent.

The ABA were forced to go away and draw up a more comprehensive and transparent application, but when it was resubmitted, Sport England still weren't happy and the problem dragged on into the New Year of 1999. It wasn't until April that we heard that the ABA, having had to go away umpteen times to tighten up or revise their application, had finally got it right. One of the conditions Sport England insisted on before granting the money was that the boxers had to be represented on the board in all discussions and meetings affecting the sport, which meant that from now on the ABA would have to consult us about their plans. That, too, was a major development. Boxers were now allowed to have views – as a direct result of me lobbying the ABA and the BOA.

It would still be several months before some of the £491,000 to be awarded was made available to the boxers. This was not the fault of the lottery people, just an inevitable result of the bungled applications made by the ABA. But the delay was particularly hard on the Olympic hopefuls who had to struggle by in debt or sacrifice their training programmes in order to work; some of them couldn't afford to wait and turned pro. I myself hadn't thrown a punch for six months when the application was eventually accepted. I carried on doing some basic fitness training, but I was a long way from being fighting fit as I had devoted all my time and energy to taking up the political cause while trying to finish my degree. If I was thrown into an Olympic ring at this stage, I would probably have got mashed up by a bantamweight. (I had told people that I would not box again until the Lottery issue and the political problems were solved, but the truth of the matter was that I couldn't have boxed anyway because I had to undergo a further hernia operation. I kept the surgery quiet as best I could in order to keep up the pressure in the battle for amateur boxing.)

When I finally hang up my gloves, no matter what I might have achieved as a professional, I will look back on my role in championing the cause of British amateur boxing as one of the proudest aspects of my career. I like to think that the march on Parliament was one of the most important episodes in the history of the sport in Britain, when the athletes rose up and made a difference. It was the culmination of months of lobbying, and we took our cause right up to the front door of British government. I showed that we were prepared to take direct action and not just fire off the odd begging fax or letter as had been the case in the past. I had struck a decisive blow for the cause of amateur boxing, not just for the short term but for long into the future, because the government had finally recognised the worthiness of the sport and set a precedent for later administrations. It will now be extremely difficult for the government to drop its commitment or reduce the level of funding for future events, meaning that British boxers should now be able to compete with the rest of the world on more level terms.

My own personal finances were also beginning to improve at this time. The police had paid Hazel and me the agreed compensation and the £27,000 I was awarded allowed me to pay off my student loans, my overdrafts, my credit cards and all the money lent me here and there by friends. In total I now owed £15,000 and without the payout I would have been in serious financial trouble as I began my training for the Olympics. In January 1999, the BOA awarded me a scholarship which amounted to about £700 per month. For the first time in my life, I could wake up in the morning or go to bed at night not worrying about where the next tenner was coming from or fretting about the bailiffs bashing on the door of the flat I was sharing with my brother Terry in Kingsbury, threatening to take possession of my furniture.

By the late summer the lottery money had been released, so I found myself in the welcome position of being double-funded: by the BOA and by Sport England.

During my preparations for the World Championships in Houston, Texas, in September, I had received my first real offer to turn professional. Frank Warren, Britain's biggest promoter, offered me £100,000 just as a signing on fee. There were other approaches, but Warren was the only one who put his money where his mouth was. It was tempting, particularly as the row over the funding rumbled on for months and there was always the possibility it might never materialise. I went away and thought about Warren's offer for a week. More money that I could dream of at this stage in my life could have been sitting in my bank account within a couple of days, plus the prospect of a lot more to come.

I have to admit that there were times during that week as I padded around my flat in Kingsbury when I was just seconds away from picking up the phone and ringing back Frank and saying, 'OK, it's a deal.' But each time I stopped myself and now I am very glad that I did. Two things kept nagging at the back of my mind: first, for years I had lain awake at night dreaming about standing on the podium in Sydney. How would I feel about myself if I was prepared to throw that away at the first offer of good money? Money has never been everything to me. If it comes, that's great, but I have never been a greedy type. I was never one of those guys who always wanted to have a flash car. Cars get rusty and end up on the scrap heap, but an Olympic gold medal is something that I could cherish for the rest of my life, with or without a personal fortune. I would always be 'Audley Harrison, Olympic gold medallist'.

Secondly, if it was just a question of money, an Olympic gold medal could be worth up to a hundred times that original offer. If I joined Frank Warren at that stage of my career I would have been just another journeyman pro and, apart from anything else, I still had a great deal to learn. I wasn't ready for that step up. Everyone kept reminding me (and they still do) that time was not on my side after taking up boxing so late, but I had my career mapped out in my head and I didn't feel under any pressure in that respect. After Sydney I would turn twenty-nine which, by my reckoning, gave me six years to launch an assault on winning world heavyweight championship titles. So after a week of agonising I called Frank Warren back and told him my mind was made up. It was Sydney gold or bust.

Before I could return to full-time training, there was the small matter of completing my degree at Brunel University. I had been due to graduate in 1998, but because of my boxing commitments I had had to put my studies on to the back burner. I had failed one of my modules and had not had time to complete my ten thousand word thesis, so the university gave me an extension which allowed me to concentrate on winning gold in Kuala Lumpur and finishing my degree when I got back.

In those six months after the Commonwealths I finished all the outstanding work and I graduated in May 1999 as Audley Harrison BSc (Hons, 2:2). It was a very proud moment for me as my father and brothers watched me, dressed in gown and mortar board, walk up to accept my certificate. I'm sure there were a lot of lecturers who didn't give me a chance of passing because of my attendance record. Partly because of my other commitments and partly because I'm not really a bookworm, you didn't see me in the library every day – or even every week, for that matter. But I knew what I had to do to pass, and did no more than I needed to. When I was called up to receive my degree, and as I walked back to my seat, I flashed a cheeky grin at all the lecturers and tutors who had doubted my ability and commitment. I had been in tougher spots than being a few weeks late with my essays, and I always knew I could make up the ground. There had been problems all the way, mainly because of the time I had to devote to boxing, but it was a sweet moment. The degree and my qualifications from Conel were not just pieces of paper: I learned a lot of things that were relevant to my career as a boxer and to someone involved in running sports. The leisure management side of it has proved to be especially helpful since I turned pro and has helped me look after myself outside the ring. I knew what I was doing when I set up my own company, and I didn't need to turn to outsiders and run the risk of being exploited. I knew how businesses worked.

It had been a great six months: my debts were paid off, the lottery money had been won and I had graduated from university. The only problem was that I was completely out of shape physically, and by the time I eventually returned to the gym at the end of June I only had a few months to get myself sorted for the World Championships. England had never won a medal at the World Championships, but after my Commonwealth success I was confident that I would be the first – a little too confident, as it turned out.

I hadn't been near a boxing gym and I was a massive 19½ stone – over 2 stone heavier than in Kuala Lumpur and the heaviest I had ever been – when I put my boxing gloves back on for the first time in nine months. I felt like a lorry. I worked flat out to get my weight down and managed to shed about a stone, but I wasn't anywhere near 'boxing fit' by the time we flew out. In the short time available I trained to lose weight rather than to compete: all I was doing was physical conditioning and there was virtually no technical input. To the man on the street I would have looked fit, but I was ring-rusty and I was going to regret entering the tournament. I also made the mistake of doing all my training in pro gyms, sparring with Julius Francis, Harry Senior and Herbie Hide, the former world champion. Without realising it, in the rush to get into shape I quickly evolved into a pro boxer in terms of body condition. In amateur boxing you need to be quick and lithe on your feet and with your fists, so you can make quick raids on your opponent, score a couple of points and get out. But the pro training turned me into a lumbering hulk with a massive upper body and slow feet – all power, no speed and agility.

Stupidly, I put my neck on the block by telling everyone I was going to win the gold medal when the sensible thing would have been either to stay at home or to go there and play down my expectations of a medal. I should have told myself – and the press – that I was going in order to get as much competitive experience as possible against the best amateurs in the world. But the problem was that I had started to believe my own hype. The Commonwealth gold and the political triumph of getting the National Lottery money sorted out had gone to my head and I was too big for my boots. I tipped myself for glory, but it all blew up in my face. We all make mistakes in our life and this was one of mine, but I learned from it and in a way it was just the kick in the pants I needed to re-focus my mind on the challenge of winning gold in Sydney.

We went back to Tallahassee for more warm weather conditioning, but the trip was a disaster. Because the Lottery money had only just come through, no plans had been made and our preparations were done in a desperate rush. For a long time we did not know if we would be going to Houston at all, and then all of a sudden everything had to be dropped and we were herded on to the plane and flown out there. Normally, for a major tournament like the World Championships, there would be two or three training camps, each about a fortnight long. This time we had just one and it was so hastily arranged that the programme was all over the shop. The only good thing about Tallahassee was that Brian Pollard wasn't there. The team manager on this occasion was Clive Howe, a long-serving and top official in national and international amateur boxing. He was about seventy years old, knew everyone worth knowing in world amateur boxing and pulled some weight. But although he was very much part of the establishment, he had the boxers' interests at heart.

Despite the rush and my poor physical condition I still arrived at the George R. Brown Convention Center in Houston with high hopes that I might become England's first-ever medallist at these championships. I swaggered around with my mobile phone, I had 'Audley Harrison' T-shirts made up and sent out press releases on the headed paper of my new PR company Advantage (now called Octagon). I had signed up with them not long after the Commonwealth Games when they approached me at a conference for the sponsors of the British Olympic Association, who had asked me to give a speech. They were a little surprised to discover that I didn't have an agent and within a couple of days we were in negotiations. They seemed to have an impressive set-up with a number of top athletes on their books, many of them Americans, but also the England cricketer Darren Gough and the Russian tennis star Anna Kournikova.

I had lost the plot a little in Houston and it was a bit pathetic. I'm not proud of the way I conducted myself at this point of my career. I even wore one red boot, one blue boot – anything to get people's attention.

I got drawn in the first round against a tough opponent from Uzbekistan called Lazizbek Zokirov (try saying that with your gum shield in) who had been impressive in winning the World Cup in China the previous year. I had seen three of my England team-mates lose in the same ring earlier that day, and I was determined not to make it a fourth straight defeat for the squad. I was expecting a really difficult fight, but I found it easy to open him up and I caught him with a series of strong right jabs and left hooks. Despite being in pretty average condition I battered him – just broke him up round after round. He had to have two standing counts before I won 13–2 to reach the quarter-finals, just one fight away from securing England's first-ever medal.

I got even more confidence from that fight, which was the last thing I needed at this point. It was caution rather than confidence I could have done with. I was starting to think I was invincible when I was drawn against an overweight Turk called Siren Samil in the last eight. After my first fight I got out of the ring and saw him getting ready to go in and I started smiling to myself. I stuck around to have a look and check out his opponent, a German soldier called Cenigz Koc (Koc would play a role in my pre-Olympic year, but more of that later). I walked off after the Turk had won, thinking there was no way this boy had a chance of beating me. But he was actually a very experienced fighter who had been at the top of the world scene far longer than I had, although not at lower weights.

Later I watched the whole of his fight on video, but didn't really analyse it properly like I normally would. I had prepared for my fights meticulously since my early career, and I always tried to get hold of videos of my opponents even if it meant paying people out of my own pocket. I never left anything to chance, but on this occasion I did, because I was feeling so full of my own hype. I just watched the video as I walked around the room, chatting on the phone. To me the Turk just looked like a clown in shiny shorts. I made the elementary mistake of failing to give him respect, and in doing so didn't pick up on one very important aspect of his style which would cost me dearly. He was little for a super-heavyweight, so he had to be resourceful and clever in order to overcome more powerful opponents.

I wasn't the only one who thought I would walk the fight. Even *Boxing News*, one of the most respected boxing journals, felt confident enough to announce 'Harrison on the Verge of History' because they assumed I would take this guy to school and secure a bronze. That issue came out a few days before the fight and just added to the sense of complacency I was already carrying around with me from the moment I arrived in Houston.

When I stepped into the ring with his guy, I looked at him and thought, 'You're a little fat Turk and you're getting knocked out.' But after a minute or so I realised I was totally unprepared to deal with his weird, disruptive style. From the first bell he kept his glove hovering and twitching in front of my face, obscuring my line of sight so that I couldn't throw a punch without the risk of exposing myself. It was a highly effective tactic (even if it hadn't been lifted straight from the Marquess of Queensberry's rules on the spirit of the noble sport) and it completely threw me. Not since I fought the squaddie Danny Watts in Aldershot barracks about four years earlier had I felt so tactically helpless. I had no game plan to beat this guy. As he fiddled around I couldn't get at him, and I lost the first two rounds. By the fourth I was desperate. I knew I was losing and in danger of an embarrassing exit, so I just went at him and tried to overwhelm him. I caught him with three clean punches and thought I had scraped it with a bit to spare. But the judges awarded him a 4–3 victory. I hadn't fought well, but if you watch it on video you will see that in the last round we were level at 3–3 before I landed three clean punches and he landed none. You can count the punches. Although I fought very badly, I thought I'd done enough to win; but the decision didn't go my way.

It is a universally accepted fact that there is a lot of corruption in international amateur boxing and bad decisions are made. But I deserved to lose because of my bad preparation and my cocky attitude. Incredibly, this Turkish guy went on to beat the

Italian Paolo Vidoz in the semis before taking the title. Nobody, including me, could believe it. He's a pro now, but in the unlikely event that I meet him again in the ring, he will be lying flat on his back barely before he has had time to put his gum shield in.

When I got back to England I felt ashamed of myself, both for the way I had prepared for the tournament and even more so for the way I had carried myself. I had let myself down, but I had also let down a lot of people who had put their faith in my abilities, including the British press. I immediately sent out a press release apologising for my performance and promising there would never be a repeat of what had happened in Houston. I took it on the chin and knew I had screwed up.

In a way it was good that I suffered this setback, because it snapped me out my complacency and made me realise how much work I needed to do for the Olympics. There was a lot of hype around me after the Commonwealths – because Britain had had virtually no success at amateur level for decades I made a bit of stir. But the problem was that I started believing all the hype myself. I thought I was bloody marvellous. The truth of the matter was that at that stage I was just a good boxer with a lot of talent who had won a Commonwealth gold. Full stop. I was not the finished article by any means and I began to realise that I had to knuckle down or I could end up looking like an idiot. I had to deliver with my gloves, not my mouth. It's no good talking a great fight, then getting battered in the ring. You look daft, and the next thing you know you're a has-been. The problem is that when everyone tells you that you are wonderful, it is easy to start believing it all. You are flattered and you start thinking, 'Well, maybe I *am* pretty cool' and then the concentration level begins to dip and you don't train so hard, and you think that natural talent alone and reputation will be enough to see off your opponent. But my experience at the World Championships taught me that I would have to be relentless if I ever wanted to achieve my dream of becoming Olympic champion. Relentless in my training, relentless in my concentration in the ring and relentless in my monastic self-discipline. I would not ease up until that gold medal was safely around my neck.

# CHAPTER 7

# A PERIOD OF QUALIFIED SUCCESS

The qualifying process for the Olympics was a deeply frustrating and depressing experience that highlighted everything that seemed to me wrong with international amateur boxing and everything that was inept about the England management. My participation in Sydney was almost in jeopardy and my relationship with the England management deteriorated so badly that, after a whole series of bust-ups, the British Olympic Association had to intervene to try and restore order on several occasions. Unfortunately, despite their best efforts, the problems continued right up to the eve of my first fight in Sydney and almost cost me a medal.

There were just a hundred places available for all of Europe's boxers, and these days it is much harder to qualify following the break-up of the Soviet Union (and, to a lesser extent, Yugoslavia) as there are now over a dozen more federations with their own contingent of boxers. Before, there would be just twelve boxers from the Soviet Union; now you have twelve from Russia, twelve from Ukraine, twelve from Uzbekistan, twelve from Kazakhstan, twelve from Belarus and so on. The amateur boxing rings of Europe were swamped in the 1990s, making it much tougher to qualify. Also, the sheer size of the qualifying field makes it easier for a dodgy decision to pass unnoticed in a mass of statistics, where a few years ago it would have stood out more. As in any walk of life, there may be an element of unconscious bias going on: not blatant cheating, but more a case of judges instinctively leaning towards their natural allies. Eastern European judges may tend to favour eastern European fighters, an English judge may favour a Welsh, Scottish or Irish fighter, Central Americans may lean towards other Central Americans.

I knew the qualifying process, which began in the second half of 1999, was going to be fraught with risk, but in my first attempt to reach Sydney I could have no complaints. I was beaten fair and square by the Russian Alexei Lezin 6–1. It was an honest fight, and he deserved to win on the night. There was nothing particularly interesting about the manner of my defeat. He was on form and I wasn't.

My second attempt at qualification was in Istanbul, where I lost 6–1 to the German Cenigz Koc. This time I thought I had walked it by more than 10 points. At the end of each round my corner kept telling me I was down but I thought this was just a bit of kidology on their part to keep the pressure up right to the end. When it was announced that I had lost, I was so surprised that I immediately presumed that they had got the two of us the wrong way round and that it was me who had won 6–1. I couldn't work out where I had gone wrong so I investigated the records. As I explained earlier, to score a point, three of the judges have to press their button within a second of each other after a clean punch. There are five judges, and the records show that for this fight I scored heavily with three of them, but when the scores were combined I don't make any impact. In the heat of the moment, I realise mistakes can happen but I really thought I had done the business this time. You can imagine how frustrating it feels to really think you've won a fight, only to find out the decision has gone the other way.

I was beginning to feel concerned about the qualification process. The prestige of winning an Olympic medal has created a massive competitiveness amongst the main boxing nations and some federations, particularly those in eastern Europe, may employ any means to ensure that their boxers get to the Games. In addition to the glory that it brings to a country and its international standing, a gold medal can also put boxers in line for a highly lucrative professional career. With forty European countries now scrapping over just a hundred places for the Olympics finals, there may be all sorts of things taking place. At these qualifying events there are many characters hanging around in the shadows and the rumour mill goes into overdrive. You hear about people being given Rolex watches, lavish dinners being laid on and knocks on hotel doors in the middle of the night. In 1996 a high-ranking Russian boxing referee never made it to the Atlanta Olympics because he was tortured and shot dead in his bath in his Moscow apartment. Two other Russian boxing officials also became victims in a lethal struggle for power in Russian boxing.

In another bout in Istanbul, a boxer was ordered out of the ring by his trainer. I know Tony Burns, my coach at Repton who has trained nine Olympic boxers, was taken aback by a number of other decisions. It's inevitable that you begin to worry when you're really hoping to win Olympic glory.

At around the same time the investigative journalist Andrew Jennings, who exposed the corruption in the Olympic movement in his book *The Lords of the Rings*, said the Russian mafia were mobilising for Sydney. In the run-up to the Games several newspapers claimed the Russian mobsters already knew the winners of most of the boxing divisions. I even read one report urging punters not to put a single penny on me because the Russians would see to it that I would not win. The Russians had apparently earmarked the boxers they wanted to win gold so that they could launch them as pros after Sydney and make millions from them. Anyone involved in international amateur boxing knows that these stories are a lot more substantial than mere rumours. Everyone remembers the Seoul Olympics in 1988 when Roy Jones, one of the best pound-for-pound boxers of his generation, lost the gold medal to an unknown Korean, Park Si-Hun, whom no one ever heard of again, despite out-punching him 4–1.

When we got back to England I went to see Kevin Hickey, the technical director of the British Olympic Association. I have a great deal of respect for Hickey, as I have for the whole of the BOA. He has an impressive track record in sport and in sports administration, and was British boxing coach at five Olympics and five Commonwealth Games. The BOA, mean-while, is a highly efficient, supportive organisation which puts the welfare of the athletes above all.

Hickey just sat me down and asked, 'Do you still think you have the ability to qualify?'

I said, 'Of course I do.'

And he just said, 'Go out there and steamroller your way to gold in Sydney.'

The qualifying process was not the only source of frustra-tion. My relationship with the England camp, and with my trainer, Terry Edwards, in particular, was getting worse by the session. The England authorities were starting to panic because they thought the lottery money would be stopped if Britain didn't have any qualifiers for Sydney. It wouldn't reflect well on the amateur boxing set-up in Britain, headed up by Ian Irwin and Edwards, if we had no boxers there. As each qualifying tournament went by and still no Brit had booked his place they got more and more agitated.

If I needed any further motivation to qualify, it was provided by a handful of critics in the press who started writing off my chances. There is never much national newspaper coverage of these qualifying tournaments and generally it's just the results, if anything, that get printed up back home. So as far as most journalists were concerned I had simply lost my first two qualifiers – they hadn't seen what I thought was a good performance against Koc, even though I'd lost. My disappointing performance at the World Championships had generally lowered people's expectations of me, and when I set off for my third qualifier people, understandably maybe, thought I must be struggling.

Nothing could have been further from the truth, and by the time I arrived at my third qualifying tournament, in Halle in Germany in March, I felt like a raging bull. I could have fought two boxers at once I was so pumped up with frustration and urgency. I didn't have any sex for three weeks before the qualifiers and took out all my pent-up emotions on my opponents. I think it's a bit of an old wives' tale that sex on the eve of a big event saps your energy and undermines your performance. I've indulged in sexual activity before a fight and I can't say that I noticed the difference physically. But what is probably true is that by not having sex you are sacrificing something, and so you feel disciplined on the day of your fight. To have sex implies that your mind is not entirely focused on your fight. It is a pleasure, and pleasure is not something you build into your pre-fight programme alongside sparring, circuit training, heavy bag work, weights sessions, pulling cars and running. Add sex to that list and somehow it doesn't all quite add up.

My relationship with Terry had deteriorated slowly over the previous eighteen months or so to the point where there was simply no meaningful contact between us. The first time I began to question whether our relationship was going to be a happy one occurred when I did the ABA assistant coach's course which was being run by Terry. I had taken along Errol, my assistant at the Brunel University club, who had been working with me in the gym for a couple of years. Errol was more into martial arts than boxing but he understood boxing and learned a lot with me while working in the gym. When Terry failed Errol in the practical part of the course (which was basically just padwork and something Errol had been doing more than competently at Brunel) I was more than a little surprised because I couldn't see what he had done wrong. When I confronted Terry, he didn't really give me an answer, saying only that he failed. I was irritated and started to question whether Terry was someone I wanted to work with.

I had three fights in Halle and before my second, against a Czech fighter, although both Ian and Terry were there, I felt like I was on my own. I don't really blame Ian Irwin because there is no malice in the man, but in my experience he couldn't handle it when the pressure was really on. His reaction was to retreat rather than to take positive, decisive action. I had lost all respect for Edwards by this stage. We had had a number of flare-ups and I didn't want him anywhere near me. He wasn't the right coach for me and the worst thing was that I felt I never got constructive feedback and criticism from him.

At the Commonwealth Games his indifference turned into something more confrontational. After winning the gold I was being interviewed on television and I took the opportunity to thank all the people who had helped me in my success. I singled out Tony Burns from Repton because it was him I worked with on a day-to-day basis and from whom I learned the most. The England camps only happened over a weekend period four or five times a year and I would be lying if I said I had ever felt a dramatic improvement in my game after one of them and so I never mentioned the England coaches in my tribute, I just thanked the whole national set-up. When the interview was over, Terry was furious and said to me sarcastically, '"Thank you very much, Tony fucking Burns." I've been holding pads for you for the last two months and you've been bashing hell out of my hands. How come I never got a thank you? All Tony Burns does is walk around with a fag in his hand.'

I tried to explain that being a good trainer involved more than just padwork; that Tony was special to me because of what I'd learned from him about man management and technique development. Right up to the Olympics this became a stock taunt for Terry, 'Well we all know what Audley is going to say if he is successful in Sydney – "Thank you Tony Burns."' It was almost as if he was envious of Tony for the great respect I had for him.

The mood in the camp was low and there were all sorts of tensions behind the scenes. One development in particular infuriated me. Before going out to Halle, I had contacted the BOA about getting a physiotherapist sent out. I had been struggling with hand and shoulder injuries and I didn't want to take any risks at this stage and felt it was crucial that I was in the best possible shape. Knowing from past experience that there was no chance of the England management sorting it out, I went straight to the BOA, who were happy to oblige. The physio was a girl called Caroline, but as soon as she arrived the coaches took her under their authority even though they didn't even know she was coming out until the last minute.

After training or a fight Caroline would come into the changing room or my bedroom to give me a massage, but on each occasion she was accompanied by one of the junior trainers, who would just stand there while she worked on me. During my massage sessions I like to use the quiet time to relax or practise my visualisation techniques, but he kept asking Caroline loads of questions and even tried to massage and probe me himself. I kept telling him to get lost and leave me alone to relax and think and eventually after the third or fourth occasion he did. It was deeply irritating and I felt annoyed that my peace of mind was being toyed with.

At these international events there are generally two rings, one red, one blue, because there are so many fights to get through. The programme in Halle included both Olympic and European championship qualifiers and one of my fights coincided with another involving an English boxer, the middleweight Carl Froch, who was fighting for a place in the Europeans. I had already qualified for the Europeans when I beat the Italian Paolo Vidoz in the final of the Acropolis Cup in Athens at the end of 1999. Vidoz was the unofficial world number one at the time after beating Lezin and the Cuban Alexis Rubalcaba earlier in the year. None of us boxers really cared about the Europeans – all we were interested in was getting to Sydney. What happened before my second fight I took as a personal insult and was the turning point in my relationship with Ian and Terry.

Ian, the head coach, went off to oversee Carl's fight and left me in my corner with Terry and one of the other boxers, Steve Bell. Ian knew my relationship with Terry was getting worse and worse but left him with me, and he also knew that getting a boxer to the Olympics was far more important than getting one into the European Championships. I made up my mind there and then that if I was ever going to win an Olympic gold I would have to do it on my own, with no help from the back-up staff. I sat in the changing room, put on my headphones and listened to some music to get myself psyched up and into the zone. When it was time to go out for the fight, Terry

Edwards came in. He didn't say one word to me. We walked out into the arena and he put my gum shield in. There was total silence. Carl's fight finished early and Ian came over for my second round, but the insult had already been committed. It was too late.

The morale in the England camp had now sunk to new depths following an incident earlier in the day during a fight involving Andrew Wallace, another Repton boxer. The rest of the team were ringside to cheer him on. As David Haye, England's heavyweight, stood up and shouted encouragement: 'Come on, Wallace, get stuck in, that's the way, throw the upper cut...' Terry Edwards spun round and started screaming at him in front of everyone. 'Shut your bloody mouth, you idiot. I'm in the corner not you,' he shouted. If confirmation was needed that there was a massive division between us and them, Edwards provided it with that outburst. He humiliated David in front of the all the other boxers and coaches watching on that side of the ring. It was completely out of order, and you could see some of the other boxers around us sniggering to each other as this Little England farce unfolded. What kind of a team was this where you couldn't even support your colleagues? David was really put out by Edwards' behaviour and it badly affected the morale of the team, so fragile already. But although all the boxers to a man were fed up with the way things were being run, they were too frightened to speak their minds in case they were thrown off the team.

Carl Froch was the one who suffered most in Halle. He was only there for the European qualifiers and his Olympic bouts were to be held the following week at the Multi-Nations in Liverpool. To qualify for the European Championship finals you only had to reach the semis of the qualifying event, and what all the other nations were doing was pulling their boxers out once they had done that. They knew the upcoming

Olympic bouts were just around the corner and didn't want to expose their boxers to the risk of being knocked out and the resultant automatic twenty-eight-day lay-off. But not the England management. When Carl reached the semis he too wanted to pull out, but the management ordered him to carry on fighting. It seemed to me that they just wanted a medal and they weren't putting Carl's interests first, which I thought was disgraceful and inexcusable. Carl was so upset that he came to me in tears. I went and told Ian that I thought it was out of order and he should let Carl make up his own mind about what was good for him and his career. The next morning when I went down to the weigh-ins at the venue I saw Ian, Terry and the manager Harry Pritchard with Carl trying to persuade him to go through with the European fights. Carl lacked a bit of confidence in himself at the time and, though he looked visibly upset, he stepped up on to the scales and that was that.

I was fighting later that night for my Olympic qualification, the most important night of my career so far, but there I was acting as counsellor/psychologist/agony uncle for a distressed team-mate. I should have been concentrating on my quest to reach Sydney but instead, thanks to the England management, I spent the day trying to get Carl's head right. The boy was so depressed about the way he had been treated that his mind was now not on the fight, so I spent two hours talking him up, trying to lift his spirits. It was a dangerous situation for him, because if his mind was not on the job he could get knocked out. In the end he went out there and battered the guy, but the point was that in my view he should never have been risked in the first place and the management should never have treated him like they did. After all the fuss we had kicked up, the management eventually let him pull out of the final. When he went up to collect his silver medal all the team were shouting and cheering for him.

It was against this background that I went into my third bout in my third qualifying tournament, but to some extent the rows with the management had concentrated my mind on the task ahead. All the frustrations that had mounted over the previous weeks erupted in the ring and resulted in a crushing 14–2 win over the Belarussian Sergei Detschkov. I was the first British boxer to qualify and after nine years of hard graft on the amateur circuit I was now just three or four fights from an Olympic gold medal.

I had come the hard way, battling against a string of injuries including a nose operation to improve my breathing, three hernia operations, a ruptured knuckle hood and torn tendon, stress fractures in both feet and a torn ligament in the shoulder. I had fought 12 Olympic and European contests in all – but I saw the tough qualifying process as a positive because I would arrive in Sydney that much more experienced and battle-hardened. I had left nothing to chance after my first two attempts and there was no way I was going to let my rivals – or the judges – deny me. There was an historical precedent which allowed me to draw some comfort from the struggle of the qualifying process. Britain's last boxing Olympic gold thirty-two years earlier had been won by middleweight Chris Finnegan, a west London bricklayer by trade, who almost didn't make it to the Mexico Games. He suffered an eye injury before his qualifier and was so upset about the prospect of missing out on the Games that he went on a two-week drinking binge that ended in a brush with the law. But he was given one more chance when he managed to secure a box-off, which he won to book his flight to Mexico.


I had decided that Edwards would never stand in my corner again. Halle had been the final straw. I felt he was not up to the job of steering me to gold because I had learned all I could from him and we no longer got on personally.

In Germany I decided to confront the establishment about all the problems that had come to a head over the previous few weeks. I had a meeting with Edwards, Irwin and Pritchard, another veteran establishment figure, and told them that all the boxers were fed up with the way the team was being run and that no one was listening to our concerns. I reminded them that it was us, the boxers, who were the most important people in the sport – it was not trainers and managers who would be standing on podiums in Australia in a year's time. It was time for them to start working *for* us, and it was time to stop treating us like kids who didn't know what was good for them. Their treatment of Carl had summed up all that was wrong in the camp. 'How the hell can you expect to build up a sense of team spirit if you go around bullying vulnerable young boxers like Carl?' I shouted at the three of them. 'You're meant to be looking after this kid, not bullying him and reducing him to tears. You should be ashamed of yourselves.' Predictably, they denied everything.

I went to see Tony Burns to ask his advice about what I should do and he suggested that I have another chat with Ian Irwin and try and sort out the problem once and for all. Ian had recently become performance director for the new Lottery-funded World Class Performance Plan, but rather than give up his role as head coach he decided to take on both posts which in my view was too much work and commitment for one man and I believe both posts suffered as a result. It would turn out that I would have several more meetings with Ian on the subject of my working relationship with Terry Edwards.

After qualifying I flew out to New York to watch the Lennox Lewis v Michael Grant fight. I wanted to start putting myself about and show my face a bit in professional circles so that, come the Olympics, potential promoters and TV networks would already know my name. I had no hesitation in selling myself at any available opportunity, so when, before the fight, I found myself in a lift with a guy from TVKO, the pay-per-view arm of the HBO network, I told him I was the favourite to win Olympic gold in Sydney. It was not technically true, but he said he would get me on television and took me into the studio. Within minutes I was being interviewed live about the fight and telling everyone who I was and how I was going to become Olympic champion and then turn pro. I barely drew breath for five minutes, and when the interview was over the presenter said, 'Wow, man, you sure can talk! You can have a job here when you stop boxing. You can talk for England.'

The guy I had spoken to in the lift turned out to be Steve Farhood, a top boxing journalist and television analyst. After the Olympics he wrote a piece in *The Ring* magazine, recounting how he had met this big-mouthed guy from England whom he had never heard of and who was telling everyone he was going to win gold. He said he thought I was just hyping myself at the time, and couldn't believe it when he saw me standing on the podium in Sydney six months later. Apparently, during my live interview, all the producers at HBO were saying to each other, 'Why the hell are we giving this guy air-time? No one in the States has a clue who he is.'

Panos Eliades, Lennox's promoter, at least knew who I was and he was trying to sugar me while we were out there. He got me ringside seats and made sure I was well looked after for the whole weekend. After the fight I carried on making an exhibition of myself, and at the post-fight party I wandered around with my camcorder interviewing all the boxing people like Floyd Mayweather Jnr, David Reid, Fernando Vargas, Steve Collins and Wayne McCullough. I pretended I was doing a documentary for a British TV channel, and so I've got

Mayweather and all these other American boxers pointing at the camera and putting on a show saying, 'I'd just like to say thanks a lot to all my fans back in Britain. I love my British fans. I love you.' But although I was messing around having a good time in New York there was a serious point to my trip too – I took the opportunity to go down to the famous Gleesons gym and meet the trainers and boxers. I did some padwork with the trainer of Zab Judah, the light-welterweight world champion, which cost me 20 dollars but was worth every cent because I learned a few more tricks from a trainer who knew what he was doing.

The political in-fighting continued behind the scenes right up to Sydney and throughout the tournament. The next problem was the selection of the back-up team. Originally, the BABA (British Amateur Boxing Association, which is made up of representatives from England, Scotland, Wales and Northern Ireland) had selected a Welsh team manager we had never met and Ian Irwin as coach. When all the qualifiers were finished Britain had just two boxers going to Sydney: me and light heavyweight Courtney Fry, both of us Repton-based Englishmen. This back-up team was not what we wanted. Ian Irwin has some good qualities but in my opinion technically, like Edwards, he wasn't the right person to see me through the biggest event in amateur boxing. I had long stopped doing padwork with him because I didn't feel I was learning anything new from him. I needed to be learning new combinations, to be pushed much harder. The Welsh guy, meanwhile, knew nothing about us, we knew nothing about him, and as far as we knew he didn't have much pull within AIBA, the international governing body.

The whole set-up was unsatisfactory and it went ahead without any consultation with Courtney and me. In May Ian

**Inset**: Receiving an injection in my ruptured knuckle before the final, no pain, no gain.

**Main** In full battle cry... Vidoz experiences the full 'A-Force' during the Olympic semi-final.

**Above** On the front foot… battle charge… *touché*.

**Below** Reasons to be cheerful… I know the Olympic gold is mine as I finish off the Kazakhstani…

**Facing page** The moment I had dreamt about for ten years – my coach Ian Irwin had been dreaming about it for even longer!

**Above** The Boys' Club… from left, my trainers Kelvin, Wendl and Akim, head club coach Tony Burns and National coach Ian Irwin.

**Below** The class of 2000… Britain's medallists show off their spoils.

**Facing page** Time to celebrate… 'You've done your country proud my son!' Flying the flag for Britain.

**Above** A Royal encounter... meeting Her Majesty the Queen and Princess Anne at the Royal Olympic reception.

**Below** Medal man... with my MBE after the ceremony at Buckingham Palace and with my father Vincent and my brothers Rowan (left) and Terry after the trip to the Palace.

**Above** In the presence of the great man… myself, Lennox Lewis and Naseem Hamed look on as Princess Haya of Jordan presents Muhammad Ali with a birthday gift at his lavish party in Park Lane, London.
**Below left** Posing for the cameras with friends Julius Francis (left) and former world champion Lloyd Honeghan.
**Below right** A night with my confidante, Hazel.

**Above left** With my manager, Colin.
**Above right** A break from training at my luxury camp in Cornwall.
**Below left** Fully focussed as I enter Wembley for my first pro fight, cheered on by over 5,000 ecstatic fans.
**Below right** Victory!

set up a meeting with Simon Clegg, the head of the BOA, and by all accounts a man of great initiative and clout. At this meeting were Clegg, Irwin, Kevin Hickey, me, Courtney and Tony Burns, our coach from Repton. Burns is great. He'll do anything for his boxers, and it was good of him to come along to the meeting to support us. He may take the piss out of you, but the man is a boxer's dream. Tony made it quite clear that he didn't want to go to Sydney in an official capacity but would be there, as always, supporting from ringside. Courtney is a quiet, shy character who tends to clam up a bit in public or in meetings, so I did most of the talking (which is not something I need much encouragement to do). All we really wanted was a good trainer out in Sydney, someone we could learn from, who would inspire us, someone we knew and respected. Kelvin Travis was our ideal choice. The BOA agreed on a compromise whereby the Welsh manager would no longer be going, Ian would take his place and a new trainer would be named. Afterwards, I told Ian that Courtney and I would like to have Kelvin as our trainer and that under no circumstances were we prepared to work with Edwards. If we could wish only one thing for the Olympics, that was it: no Terry Edwards. I couldn't have made it any clearer to Ian, and as the months went by each time I saw Ian or spoke to him I asked him what was happening with the coaching position. But he kept avoiding the question, saying everything was under control and there was nothing to worry about it.

In the summer I turned up for a training camp at Crystal Palace before we headed off to an international meeting in Belgium. As I walked in, there was Ian standing with Terry Edwards. I couldn't believe my eyes. So I confronted Ian and asked him what the hell he thought he was doing. It was Courtney and I who were going for gold, not him, but Ian just tried to slip out of it, saying that Terry was the right man because we had worked together for so long. I replied that that was precisely the reason why I never wanted to work with him again. I suppose I should have long given up being surprised by the antics of the amateur boxing authorities, and to some extent this was just typical of the total lack of communication between us. But this new situation just beggared belief and I kept hammering away at Ian over the next few weeks to make sure that Terry would not be going to Sydney. He never gave me his word that Terry wouldn't be going – nor did he say that he definitely was. He just fudged the issue every time I raised it, saying that everything would work out fine.

The international get-together in Belgium involved France, Belgium, Turkey and Germany plus Courtney and I who were guesting for the French. We all trained and sparred together for sixteen days before a mini-tournament, also featuring an African contingent, was staged at the end. It was a largely meaningless event, but I was happy to go along to pick up some experience and see if I could learn anything new.

While we were there I had a sparring session with the German Koc, who had beaten me in my second qualifier in Istanbul. I saw the sparring sessions as a chance to work on particular areas of my game and try out new techniques. Before heading out there I had been working a lot on my stamina and defence, and so I wasn't really throwing any punches against Koc, just letting him come at me.

Between rounds Terry Edwards kept shouting at me, saying I looked terrible and that I should go back in there and bash him up. I explained what I was trying to do and that I didn't care if he was beating me up. It was the Olympics I cared about, not some minor warm-up which everyone would have forgotten about in a few weeks. It seemed to me Terry just wanted to see sweat and pride and you had to do everything

154

his way, but as far as I was concerned his way was not the right way. But we never seemed able to have a proper dialogue and I felt that whenever I said I didn't want to do something his way and suggested what I saw as a more fruitful approach, he would just dismiss it.

He was starting to drive me nuts, and unless he was thrown off the coaching team there were going to be some serious problems in Sydney. This tension wrecked all our training camps. It was a farcical state of affairs – except that there was nothing remotely funny about our medal chances being undermined by the ever worsening relationship.

Terry wasn't the only who was having a go at me during that tournament. Word got back to me that the Germans, Turks and French were all slagging me off, saying I was nothing more than a gym fighter and I had no hope in Sydney. They could slag me off as much as they liked. If they wanted to underestimate me, they did so at their own peril. I'll see you in Sydney, lads, and we'll fight with our fists.

One evening after I had boxed in two contests, beating the Nigerian Peter Samuels and losing to the German Koc, we were all sitting around a table. There was me, Courtney, Ian, Terry and few others including a guy called Roland, who was one of the sponsors of the tournament and had been driving us around during the get-together. Roland, a Belgian, began laying into me, saying he agreed that I was just a gym boxer and that he couldn't believe that someone who looked so good training could be so bad in the ring. There was no humour in his comments, he was being deadly serious but everyone – apart from myself, Courtney and Ian who looked embarrassed for me – was roaring with laughter. I felt upset by what this guy was saying. But I just bit my lip and when they had finished I just said quietly, 'Just wait till we get to Sydney.'

A good example of the difference between our Olympics

preparations and those of other nations came when we held a joint training camp with Ireland at Crystal Palace. It took place in January, and at that stage we still didn't have any boxers who had qualified for the Games. The idea was that all the boxers and trainers would work together, presumably to see if they could learn anything new. The Irish had this Cuban coach called Nicholas Cruz, who was brilliant. I learned an enormous amount from him in just two days. Some of the stuff he was showing me was amazing, a total eye-opener and a contrast with the same old technical feedback I felt I'd been getting at England camps.

But before the Irish contingent departed I took Cruz's contact numbers and a few weeks later I flew out to Dublin for the first of a couple of sessions with him. I didn't tell the England management because as far as I was concerned it was nothing to do with them. They had shown that they couldn't care less about my technical development, so it was up to me to find ways of improving myself. And if that meant flying to Ireland to be coached by a Cuban, then so be it. I was hungry to learn, and I knew that technically I was not the finished article. When I went to Sydney I wanted to have as many weapons in my armoury as I could get hold of, and unfortunately the munitions dump back in the England camp was empty.

I decided not to enter the European Championships in France in May (which I had qualified for back in September) so that I could give my lingering injuries a chance to recover. But I went to the event as a television analyst for Eurosport and had a great time co-commentating with Steve Holdsworth. While I was there I also made regular visits to a pro gym where I worked with a very good local trainer who taught me a few extra tricks. By now I felt confident that my game was slowly coming together. I had worked on eradicating the weaknesses, making the most of my strengths while picking up new ideas wherever I could. Despite the injury worries and the problems in the England camp, I felt that from a technical point of view I was starting to mature into a genuine contender for the Olympic title.

# CHAPTER 8
# CARRY ON BOXING

The British boxing team for the Olympics in 2000 consisted of Courtney Fry and myself – a sad reflection on the state of amateur boxing in the country. The Cubans were the only team with a full complement of twelve while Russia, Ukraine, Uzbekistan and Australia all had ten and Germany seven. Britain, the country that had drawn up the rules and introduced organised boxing to the wider world, was sending just the two representatives, the same pathetic number that we sent to Atlanta four years earlier. I thought that was a disgrace and it made me even more determined to make a splash in Sydney 2000 so that I could thrust amateur boxing back into the limelight.

When the boxing team set out for the Great Britain training camp on the Gold Coast of Queensland there were seven of us who took our seats on the plane: me, Courtney, Ian, Kelvin Travis, our two sparring partners, Harry Senior and Andrew Lowe, and my biggest headache, Terry Edwards. Kelvin would be with us at the camp, but as things stood he would be unable to join us in Sydney as Ian and Terry had been given the only two accreditation passes. I had wanted to be pushed to the limit in training in those last few weeks, but the problem was that there were no sparring partners around who could provide me with tough enough opposition. According to the ABA rules I was only allowed to spar with other amateurs, but this was no good because there were no British boxers up to it. So I had gone to Ian and said I wanted Harry Senior, a friend of mine who had boxed for England before turning pro. I had beaten Harry in the ABA London finals all those years ago and he owed me a favour because I had offered to spar with him before his last few fights, so he was more than happy to help out. Ian was against the idea, but eventually relented and bent the rules to make sure I got what I wanted. I think he had got used to the idea that there was no point in getting involved in a battle of wills with me. I'm sure he had my best interests at heart but there was always an element of him not letting the other coaches and managers think that he was on my side.

But unfortunately no amount of pressure on Ian had managed to get Terry Edwards off the team, and once he had been given his accreditation it looked like he was there to stay. His presence was nonsensical and potentially disastrous for me. What's the point in having a guy in your corner whom you hate, and whose advice during the fight itself you don't want to hear? He would be no more than a gum shield remover. Far from there being a good working relationship between us, there wasn't one at all. Our only form of communication was bickering, which is not the most solid foundation on which to launch a bid for an Olympic gold medal.

I was going to the XXVI Olympiad, 104 years since the first modern games in Athens, but only the fifth since super-heavyweight was introduced as a category. The profile of amateur boxing has come a long way since 1896, when the organisers refused to include it on the programme, saying it was, 'ungentlemanly, dangerous and practised by the dregs of society'. Not until eight years later, in St Louis, Missouri, did it make its first appearance in the Games, but the sport had to wait until 1920 before it became a permanent fixture. Since then it has been one of the most popular disciplines in the increasingly bloated programme. The sense of history and destiny was overwhelming: if I flew back in a month's time clutching the gold medal I would have joined a list of some of the most illustrious names in heavyweight boxing history: Ali (or Clay as he was when he won the light-heavy title in Rome in 1960), Spinks, Foreman, Frazier, Mercer and Lewis.

The super-heavyweight division was expected to be one of the toughest of the twelve categories. There were fifteen other super-heavies flying out to Sydney. Twelve of them I knew all about, and I had an individual game plan to beat each of them. The other three were unknown quantities, but I would study them closely if they made it past the first round.

I was now just seven weeks away from fulfilling the dream I had been cherishing for years. Soon I would know if the huge gamble I had taken by turning down all the offers and overtures to turn pro was going to come off. The roulette wheel which had been spinning for years was now starting to slow and the ball was about to fall into place. Was it going to be my number? I was one of the most highly experienced amateurs on the world circuit and had gone from strength to strength since winning the first ABA title. My focus became even more intense when we arrived in Australia. I didn't care if I missed the 100-metre finals and I didn't care if I never left the camp or the venue and saw nothing of Australia. I wasn't going there to have fun. I had one mission: to come back with the gold medal. Of course, I wanted the rest of Team GB to succeed, but I had to concentrate on my own assignment. I couldn't let my focus start wandering from the task in hand, jeopardising years of preparations and mounting hopes.

The press had written off my chances of gold by the time we left England. For them, the fact that I had only qualified at the third attempt was proof that I was unlikely to deliver in the finals. That was fine by me. If I had gone there with everyone expecting me to win and then won, the reaction would have been 'So what?', but if no one gave me a prayer then my triumph would be all the more remarkable.

I arrived with six international titles safely stored away under lock and key back home, and when I told people I was going to win the gold (as I had done over and over again) I was never just talking a good fight and building up the hype. It was no more than a realistic assessment of my chances based on my track record as an amateur over the past four years. I knew that I would not have to fight out of my skin or punch above my weight, as it were, to win gold. I would just have to be utterly professional and focused in my approach. 'Focus' is a word bandied about so often by athletes that it has become something that many people say automatically without really knowing or caring what it means. But 'focus' for me was – and is – a very real and very important part of my preparations as well as my performance in the ring. Before I left England I read an article by Linford Christie which had some good advice: 'Go to the Olympics and expect a bronze and you'll get nothing, aim for a silver and you'll get a bronze, but aim for the gold and you'll at least get somewhere close.'

I saw my biggest rivals as the Italian Paolo Vidoz, the Cuban Alexis Rubalcaba and the Russian Alexei Lezin. It was a difficult one to call if you looked at the form book: the Russian had been knocked out by the Cuban, I had lost to the Russian, the Russian had lost to the Italian, I had beaten the Italian and the Italian had beaten the Cuban. There is no such thing as an easy fight against a Cuban. Castro's country is the great superpower of amateur boxing, and they had won eleven out of twenty-four gold medals in the last two Olympics.

Despite my underlying confidence, I still had several problems as we settled into our camp on the Gold Coast. First and foremost, there was the never-ending Terry Edwards saga which would have to be resolved before I could find the peace of mind essential to my preparations. But also, niggling away at the back of my mind, was my physical condition. I was not in as good a shape as I would like to have been. My left shoulder, which had become destabilised again and had been bothering me for five months, was the main concern. But there were also worries over my third knuckle on my left hand, my hernia – and the strains caused by my flat feet. As a big man carrying a lot of weight I have difficulties with my feet, because when I run they have to take the pressure of 18 stone-plus hammering into the ground. In July I had turned my ankle while playing in a charity football match for the British Boxing Board of Control, and had been unable to run for about five weeks. That had now cleared up, but the damaged ankle was the one I had shattered as a teenager and there was always the fear that another slip could make it flare up again. Throughout my boxing career there has never been a time when I went into competition feeling absolutely 100 per cent. It has always been a case of limiting and controlling the injuries. Thank heavens for the BOA medical staff on the Gold Coast where the doctors and physiotherapists gave me the best possible treatment and patched me up in time for the start of the tournament.

But I had at least sorted out the balance between physical strength and speed. At the World Champs I had loaded up my upper body too much, which made me slower and less supple. As an amateur you want to be quick around the ring, picking off your opponent like a fencer, not bludgeoning him necessarily. It's best to assume that a fight will go the distance, because most of them do, and therefore it's not wise to rely on being able to stop your opponent. Knockouts are extremely rare, and in all probability there would only be a couple in the hundreds of fights which would take place over the two and a half weeks of competition in Sydney.

My stamina levels were always going to be crucial at the Olympics, where I would have to be ready for four two-minute rounds, throwing a punch every two seconds if I had to. In the build-up I had started doing a lot of high-intensity cardiovascular work: shuttle runs, circuit training and weights programmes. At the same time I wanted to improve my power, because despite my size I had found that stronger opponents were able to 'back me up' and I didn't have sufficient power to resist.

Over the summer I had gone to see Pat Fox, the fitness conditioner at Wasps rugby club in London, following recommendations from several athletes. Pat was a great help and I started on a comprehensive fitness programme. I was prepared to try anything to get myself into perfect condition and as a consequence found myself in some weird situations – like pulling cars up hills with a horse girth, borrowed from the Peacock gym in Canning Town, strapped around my torso. I had also started wrestling more with my sparring partners, and after a few weeks I started to see a major improvement in my ability to resist. I was much, much stronger, and when my sparring partners started working on my body or trying to back me up, they found themselves pounding and pushing against an immovable brick wall. There were only three dedicated Great Britain training camps before the Olympics and most of the time I was training on my own and coming up with my own initiatives. In addition to working with Pat Walsh, I also did some sessions with the 400-metre runner Donna Fraser who taught me some really useful pliametric routines for leg work and speed. I also began using creatine at this stage, but I decided I would probably come off it once I arrived in Sydney. A lot of athletes don't know how to use creatine and take it all the time, but it should only be used in short bursts. Creatine is good for enhancing explosive power, and six weeks before a tournament I would start to use it for the following four weeks and then stop. Some athletes complain of side-effects like cramp and wind, but if you take lots of water with it that shouldn't happen. You also put on weight, but that wasn't a problem for me as a super-heavyweight because I could be as big as I liked. Creatine only helps athletes in high-intensity explosive disciplines like sprinting or boxing. It helps if you are doing bursts of press-ups and sit-ups or sprints but is useless for stamina purposes like long-distance running. A lot of the world's top footballers use it these days.

When we arrived in Australia I immediately contacted the country's heavyweight champion Kali Meehan, a New Zealander by birth, whom I had sparred with at a pre-Olympic training camp in Australia the year before and who was staying not far down the road from the GB camp on the Gold Coast. I now had two top-quality sparring partners to help me work on different aspects of my game in those final seven weeks before the competition began.

In one session Kali tagged me with a couple of massive blows to the head. A few months earlier I would have been in trouble after that combination, but this time I was able to stabilise myself quickly and get back after him. In fact I was really pleased with my overall performance in the session, because it showed that my new fitness regime had started to bite. Afterwards, Harry came up and told me how impressed he was by the improvements in my physical strength and my ability to absorb punishment. Kali also congratulated me, saying he would be very surprised if I didn't take gold if I boxed like that in a few weeks. But a minute or two later, as I was towelling down, Terry Edwards came over to me and said, 'You were fucking shit. You haven't got a fucking hope. You were wobbled in there and nearly got knocked out.'

I replied, 'I've just gone four rounds with a pro and I was all over him, and you seem to be the only person in the gym who couldn't see that.' I challenged Edwards by saying, 'OK, Terry, you think you know everything, you're a so-called World Class Performance coach. What else did you see in those four rounds? Come on, Terry. I want to hear your wisdom.'

Silence followed, and then he said, 'You were wobbled in there' and walked off. Brilliant.

When we got into the car to go back to the camp, Terry turned to the others and said, 'Audley was wobbled in there, wasn't he?'

Both Harry and Andrew said no. 'I thought he looked brilliant, the best I have ever seen him,' said Harry. Even Ian Irwin intervened on my side for once, pulling rank on Terry and telling him he was out of order and should shut up. I sat there in the back of the car, fuming. He had to go – he was doing my head in. But for the next three days Edwards kept going on at me like a stuck record: 'You were wobbled in there. You were wobbled in there, Harrison, and you know it. If you listen to me you won't get hit.' It was becoming personal.

I went to Ian later that day and said, 'Edwards is going to lose me a medal. I want him out of my face. What are you going to do about it?' Once again Ian didn't do anything, so I was left with no option but to go over his head and contact Kevin Hickey, someone I knew I could trust to take decisive action – he would do anything in his power to meet the demands of athletes as long as they were reasonable. As the BOA's technical director, Kevin was in charge of the whole British team on the Gold Coast and had plenty on his plate as it was, but I had reached breaking point with Edwards and I wasn't prepared to let my Olympic dream be shattered by a man who was meant to be the most important and helpful person in my team.

When I went to see Kevin, I poured out all my frustrations to him. He was furious when I told him what had been going on and immediately called a meeting with Ian and Terry to ask them what the hell was going on. As a former boxing man, he understood the significance and potential consequences of a total breakdown in the relationship between boxer and trainer. Kevin read them the riot act, saying my chances of winning the gold medal were being jeopardised. He told Terry that if he couldn't say anything positive, he shouldn't say anything at all.

Terry took him at his word, and for the final ten days on the Gold Coast not a single word passed between us. It was a ludicrous situation. Each time we went for a workout, it was like we were acting in a silent movie. We didn't even say 'Good morning' to each other, and just went through the motions in the gym. Terry had reacted to Hickey's warnings by going into a childish sulk, making the problem even worse than it was beforehand. As the days went by and my first fight at the Olympics loomed ever closer, Britain's best hope of a boxing gold in thirty-two years had been sent to Coventry by his trainer.

I told Kevin that if it was not possible to get Kelvin Travis accredited for Sydney, then I wanted Edwards out and Kelvin to be given his pass. (Getting accreditation at a major event like the Olympics is much more difficult than you might think. With almost every country in the world involved there are thousands of athletes, officials and back-up staff, and passes are at a premium.) Kevin took the matter to the Chief Executive of the BOA Simon Clegg, the man in overall charge, but he dismissed our appeal, saying he had already had to come into our sport once to sort out personnel problems and that now we would just have to deal with it ourselves. This was a major blow. I immediately told Ian that I wanted absolutely nothing to do with Edwards for the entire tournament – that he was not to come anywhere near me. That, however, would not be the end of the story.

I was a long way from being in the right frame of mind while all this crap was going on, and it was increasingly difficult to put on a brave face (and an honest one) for the television cameras and press. Whenever I was asked how my preparations were going, I would just grit my teeth, then lie through them. I had to try and switch myself off during this period, pretend that Edwards didn't exist and get on with my training programme as best I could. Courtney and I would just go down to the local youth club, where our temporary gym had been set up, and work out with our sparring partners. Kelvin would be with us for the rest of the time on the Gold Coast, but he was assigned to work with Courtney while Ian worked with me. I would have preferred to work with Kelvin, but at least I didn't want to throw Ian to the sharks just off the coast every time he came near me. Terry just hung around in my background, a silent, moody, irritating presence.

I had stopped my padwork with Ian a long time ago because I was learning nothing new. He had been good for me for a while and had taken me to a certain level, but we reached a plateau and never moved on from the basic routines we had always done. I had been working on different combinations of punches since I had worked with the Cuban Cruz. Ian was brilliant at getting you fit, but on the technical and tactical side I always preferred to work with Kelvin. Ian was always encouraging me and he definitely had my best interests at heart. I'll always like the man and I hope he doesn't take it as a mark of disrespect if I say that I simply didn't feel he offered what I needed at that time. I tried to compensate in other areas of my training, especially my bag work and shadow boxing where you didn't need anyone else to help out.

All the initiatives introduced during my training for the Olympics came from me, not from Ian or Terry. I knew I still had a lot to learn, and I had to learn it as quickly as possible. I needed feedback, fresh ideas and more imaginative training methods. I was in danger of becoming too mechanical, too one-dimensional in my style. I couldn't get enough knowledge of myself as a boxer and I tried to find new ways of seeking it out. At the end of my sessions with Ian, he would just give me a slap on the back and say, 'Well done, Audley, you did good work today.' The encouragement was nice, but it wasn't moving me forward. Earlier in the year I had started doing my own evaluations, taking videos of my competitive bouts and of some of my sparring sessions which I would then watch and analyse over and over again. I would get the videos done any way I could, even if it meant paying another boxer to act as cameraman. I developed my own marking system, where I would give myself points out of ten for various aspects of my game like footwork, head movement and jabbing.

When we arrived in Sydney, I explained to Ian what I'd been doing and told him that I now needed someone on the outside, someone objective to do my marking me for me. It was no good me doing the marking myself because you never know how subjective and accurate you're being. Ian absorbed the system into my programme, which we used to great success right up to the Olympic final. Suddenly we had an effective working relationship, because after each of my fights in Sydney we would sit down with my sheets of paper and he would say, for example, 'Head movement eight out of ten, footwork five . . .' and in our next training sessions we would get to work on my speed of footwork and so on. It was hardly revolutionary stuff, but it was the first time during my association with the national set-up that I felt I had received proper technical feedback.

We flew to Sydney ten days before the start of the Games and settled into the GB village there. Kelvin, meanwhile, had to move into some digs in a place called Bankstown, which was about an hour away from us. Terry and I, of course, had not exchanged a single word in two weeks, even though we continued to live and work under the same roof. During a bust-up at one of our training camps back at Crystal Palace he had said to me, 'If you think I'm coming to Sydney just to carry your bags and drive you around you've got another think coming, Harrison.' But that's exactly what he was doing now: carrying my bags and driving me around. He would be sitting at the wheel of the car and I would be in the back, and not one grunt of conversation took place the entire time he was in Sydney.

With just a few days to go before entering the Olympic ring for the first time, there was a bad, bad smell in the camp and it was starting to get up all our noses. The tension was also starting to affect Courtney's preparations. He is a more placid character than me and was prepared just to put up with it whatever the consequences. Unfortunately (or fortunately, depending on which way you looked at it) I am not as nice a guy as Courtney, and I was going to carry on agitating until the problem was sorted.

The situation was already a very unfunny farce, but it became pure slapstick in those last few days before the competition got underway. My first-round fight, against the highly fancied Russian Lezin, was not until the Saturday, but Courtney was drawn in one of the earlier fights, on the Wednesday. Twenty-four hours before the start of his Olympic campaign, the most important moment of his career, he started looking for Ian and Terry back in the village so that he could have his final training session. He searched for four hours but couldn't find them anywhere. Eventually he found Ian fast asleep on a bench in the international zone, suffering from seasickness. That morning he and Courtney had been on a boat in Sydney harbour to do an interview with Gary Richardson from the BBC, and the experience had wiped him out. The doctors took him back to the village and put him straight to bed, where he stayed for the rest of the day. Terry, meanwhile, had also returned to the village. So Courtney had no one to take him for his final workout, and it was left to me to take him down to the gym and supervise the training session. There we were, me holding up the pads and Courtney punching away, Britain's only two boxing representatives, without a coach in sight. In a bizarre way, it was appropriate that after all the problems we had had it should come to this, the inevitable outcome of a working relationship that had gone from bad to worse. It was symbolic of the state of amateur boxing in Britain: the boxers raring to go, but no one to lead them. Like the British soldiers in the First World War, it was a case of lions being led by donkeys. The following morning, the day of Courtney's fight, the two of them got up like nothing had happened. Not a word was ever said about it.

For the whole week we had been in Sydney I had been on at Ian about setting up a meeting with Simon Clegg to resolve the coaching problem. Ian kept saying he was going to sort it out, but nothing ever happened. I had to assume that he hadn't even tried to get in touch with Clegg because he was scared of causing a fuss, and he was probably also worried that the row would reflect badly on him as the team manager. Courtney boxed and lost. He never did himself credit and performed well below his potential. On top of everything his wife was due to give birth to their first baby in a couple of weeks' time.

After the fight I ran into Ian on the stairs and asked him if he had set up the meeting with Clegg. When he said he hadn't, I lost my rag with him. 'All right, forget it, Ian. I'm going to sort it out myself,' I told him. 'I've been trying to go about everything in the right way by going through you, the team manager, but sweet fuck all has happened and my first fight is now just three days away. This has dragged on half a year and here we are a couple of days away from the fight I've been building up for since the Commonwealth Games and nothing has happened. You're meant to be the team manager – the man managing the boxers – but you haven't managed anything with regard to this very serious problem.'

I felt sorry for Ian as I said this, but I couldn't afford to be sentimental at such a time, when my Olympic dream and my subsequent career were being threatened by his unwillingness to act on my complaints. With authority comes responsibility, and as far as I was concerned he had failed to discharge his responsibilities to me. I wanted Kelvin in my corner during my fights, and I wanted Terry out of the loop. Time was rapidly running out.

The meeting with Clegg and the two deputy chefs de mission, Louise Ramsey MBE (well deserved, I might add) and Rod Carr, took place the following day, Thursday, less than forty-eight hours before I stepped into the ring to face Lezin. I can say from hindsight, and with total honesty, that that meeting was the most important moment in my Olympic quest and, possibly, in my whole career.

There was no need for me to go into a great long account about all the circumstances leading to the meeting. My message to Clegg was simple: if Terry Edwards is in my corner, I'm not going to win the gold medal and I probably won't win a medal at all. 'I want Kelvin in and Edwards out. Edwards is a boxer's nightmare,' I said. 'This has dragged on and on and on and I've tried to avoid going over the heads of the boxing management, but I have been left with no alternative. I have asked Ian every day for weeks what he was going to do about it and he has just buried his head in the sand and done nothing. Unfortunately, if my demand is not met I will be going back to England and I will be blaming people. I will want everyone to know, so this kind of cock-up won't happen again.'

When I had finished, Clegg turned to Ian and said, 'What the hell has been going on? I've already had to come into your sport once to sort out a dispute.' (To sort out the composition of the management team.) Ian admitted that we had had 'serious differences of opinion', but that he had just hoped the problem would go away.

To which Clegg said, 'How is it going to go away if you don't address the problem?'

Clegg then asked me what I wanted and I said, 'Kelvin Travis is staying in a cheap roadside motel up in Bankstown. I want him accredited immediately and in my corner for my first fight. I wanted this a year ago, but even at this late stage it will make all the difference in the world. It will change my state of mind at a stroke from being completely frustrated and distracted to being relaxed, confident and focused on the only point of being here – to win gold.'

There was not a moment of hesitation or doubt amongst the BOA people at that meeting. They said they would do anything in their power to enhance the prospects of a British medal hope. 'Leave it to us,' said Clegg.

The next day Kelvin was in the village. All the tension in my head which had come close to erupting in that week before my first-round fight was instantly lifted. If there is one sporting institution in Britain which deserves the highest praise, it is the BOA. Of all the officials I have ever had to deal with, I have never come across any as efficient, well organised and loyal to their athletes. In every key area of their organisation, there is a highly impressive and capable and resourceful figure. I dread to think what would have happened if it had been the ABA who had had the final authority in Sydney. It is no exaggeration to say that, without the swift and decisive intervention of the BOA, then I doubt very much that I would have been on that podium on the last day of the Games. And if I hadn't been on that podium, I would have been written off as a potential force in the professional game and would have struggled to find the backing I needed to launch the final stage of my career. It is fair to assume that, if I had returned to England a virtual nonentity after losing in the first or second round, my answering machine back in north London would not have been jammed by messages from the world's leading promoters.

So Kelvin moved into the boxers' lodge and Edwards became an even more peripheral, irrelevant figure who would play no part in my bid for Olympic gold. The difference in my performance in the final few training sessions was remarkable. My confidence just soared. I had a trainer in my corner who believed in me, who shouted encouragement and lifted my spirits, a trainer who would take the piss out of me and make me laugh, a trainer who knew my strengths and weaknesses as a boxer and as a character better than anyone else in the England set-up. He would come down hard on any mistakes or sloppiness, but his criticism was always constructive. Why he couldn't have been with me six months earlier, you'll have to ask the ABA.

The amazing aspect of the whole episode is how the press never got hold of the story. It would have been easy for me to have leaked the story to a tabloid journalist or blurted it out on the BBC. If I had, the problem might have been resolved far more quickly. But I was there as part of Team GB, and the last thing I wanted to do was start rocking the boat and letting off a stink around the village. Incidents like that can influence the mood of the camp and undermine the confidence of other competitors. The questioning of the press becomes more negative and, as soon as there is one story out there like that, the journalists start rooting around for more. There is a danger that the 'story' of Britain's Games becomes the problems behind the scenes. A lone incident can trigger a whole chain of events, and it wouldn't just have been the reputation of the boxing authorities that would have suffered. You can imagine the headlines: 'Boxing medal hope Harrison at war with trainer but no one cares!'

When Jason Queally, the sprint cyclist, won the country's

first gold in the one kilometre time trial, it released a great tide of optimism throughout the village and the British press and set the tone for the rest of the Games. Everyone was saying, 'Well, if this guy most have of us have never heard of can win gold, then who knows what the rest of us can achieve?' Equally, one piece of depressing, negative news might have prompted an entirely different mood. I'm only speculating, but all these thoughts were going through my head when I wrestled with my own problem and the last thing I wanted to do was start throwing my toys around in public, upset the rest of the team and damage the reputation of the BOA, who had been nothing but magnificent towards me in all my dealings with them.

# CHAPTER 9
# LORD OF THE RINGS

O ne of the great things about representing your country in the Olympics or the Commonwealth Games is life in the village. I loved it in Kuala Lumpur, but it was even better in Australia, first on the Gold Coast then down in Sydney. It's difficult to describe the camaraderie of the athletes without it sounding like a press release from the BOA, but I will cherish my memories of those few weeks for the rest of my life. I behaved exactly as I had done in Kuala Lumpur and made it my mission to get to know every single person on the team before I had left. Once again I was the self-appointed village jester, wandering around introducing myself to people, rapping songs, building people up and generally making an exhibition of myself. Donna Fraser, the 400-metre runner, was my unofficial hairdresser out there. I had had the rainbow look with the coloured rubber bands put in before setting out, but after a couple of weeks it needed redoing and so Donna became my fashion stylist for the Games. My brothers and Hazel, who had flown out separately, had arranged for a load of T-shirts to be made which they would wear around the venue and distribute to the British fans. There were three shirts with different slogans: 'Audley

Harrison Man On A Mission', 'Audley Harrison No Fear No Pain Just Glory' and 'H-Bomb The Time For Talking Has Stopped'.

When we moved down to Sydney the boxers and badminton players were put in the same apartment and I shared a room with Courtney Fry. I had known Courtney from Islington before he followed me to Repton, where there were more chances for him of fighting abroad. One quiet introvert, the other loud exhibitionist, we complement each other well and it was good having him around. I dread to think what the atmosphere would have been like if it had been just Terry, Ian and me in an apartment together. Although Courtney is three years younger, our careers make for similar reading. He was ABA champion in 1996, which I was in 1997; we were both champions in 1998, and went on to win Commonwealth gold later that year. Even our records were similar. He had won 43 out of 52 fights, while I had won 52 from 60. And despite our different characters, we share one trait – neither of us is frightened by performing on the big stage.

I almost ended up on the biggest stage of all when I came within a whisker of winning the athletes' vote for the person to carry the Union Jack at the opening ceremony. I was second choice behind the rower Matthew Pinsent, and when Simon Clegg came and congratulated me he told me it was a very close-run thing. I felt flattered that so many people in the camp should plump for me even though this was my first Olympics. It would have been an amazing honour to walk out into the Olympic Stadium with every country on the planet tuned in. Hundreds of millions of people from Greenland to Venezuela, Tahiti to the Falkland Isles were watching that ceremony. The Olympics truly does reach places that other events get nowhere near. At the announcement of our flag carrier I had a good banter with the Princess Royal, the patron of the BOA, and the next day I was told she wanted to have lunch with me and Courtney in the village. I've got a lot of time for the Princess. She's very down-to-earth and straight-talking and throughout lunch she made everyone laugh by taking the mick out of my hairstyle. She said she had never been to a boxing match so I invited her to come along to my first fight. I was only joking, but she said she would love to and promised she would be there.

Some of the athletes were really upset because they were not allowed to attend the ceremony on the grounds that it would be too tiring, and it was only those who would not be competing in the first few days who were chosen to go. Afterwards everyone agreed that the BOA was right to impose the restrictions, because we were all stiff as planks the following morning. Just standing around for a few hours is far more draining than you might have thought, and I'm glad I didn't have to box the next day because I would have been creaking like an old man. The ceremony was a fabulous occasion and the sounds and images made us all feel we were involved in something really special. Sometimes these ceremonies are just plain embarrassing – giant chickens playing football with Diana Ross and that kind of thing – but even the most cynical had to concede that Sydney's was truly spectacular.

The mood in the British camp was electrified on the opening day of the Games when Queally won his gold. Word spread around the village like a bushfire . . . and then after about half an hour everyone started asking, 'Who the hell is Queally?' No one was more surprised than me, because I thought I had introduced myself to every last member of the team. We had all been given a directory of Team GB which contained pictures and details of all the British athletes, so I went back to my room to see what Queally looked like so that I could go and congratulate him. That evening I sought him out around the village to applaud his achievement, and I wasn't the only one – there were dozens of others from all different disciplines giving him a pat on the back. The guy had only taken up cycling a couple of years earlier after a chance trip to the Manchester Velodrome and here he was, the centre of British attention, after wiping the floor with all the pre-tournament favourites. Everyone had been looking to the triathlete Simon Lessing for Britain's first gold, but then Queally's arrived out of the blue and the news crackled around the camp. Any gold would have given the whole team a boost, but the fact that it had been achieved by a virtual stranger made the impact even greater because it made all the athletes believe anything might be possible at these Games.

The boxing was to take place at the Exhibition Halls in Darling Harbour, smack in the centre of town. With a capacity of ten thousand, it was the largest of all the venues after the Olympic Stadium. For the first two rounds the auditorium would be partitioned, with fencing taking place on the other side, but for the semis and the finals the whole arena would be dedicated to boxing.

My first-round fight could not have been tougher. Lezin had beaten me fair and square to qualify for the tournament in Tampere, Finland, and he was also a former world champion, the current European title holder and one of the clear favourites here in Sydney. But I had done an enormous amount of work since he had beaten me and felt like twice the boxer I had been a year earlier.

Kelvin and Ian would be in my corner, and we knew I had to get out of the blocks quickly because when judges fall into a scoring pattern they tend to stick with it. I had studied these scoring patterns in a fair amount of detail and had come up with a system that I hoped would improve my chances. You are fighting not just another boxer but also a fallible scoring system. I planned to throw fewer but better quality punches so that they would be as plain as day for the judges to see and then open up with punches in bunches. I also knew I had to come out and bully him from the start, because he likes to dance around a bit and is not so good if you pin him down and start pressurising him. He likes the freedom of the ring, and I wanted to close him off wherever possible.

I felt good as I walked out and saw all the Union Jacks, and when the music struck up I started dancing. I was surprised by how many people there were in the crowd for the first rounds and even more taken aback to see the Princess Royal there, just as she had promised she would be. Evander Holyfield, the former world heavyweight champion, was also in the crowd. The time for talking had stopped. As I stood in that ring before the first bell rang out I realised it was nine years since I had taken up boxing and now, with each fight consisting of four two-minute rounds, I was a maximum of just 32 minutes away from winning an Olympic gold. First, though, there was the small matter of seeing off one of the best amateur super-heavyweights on the planet.

Everything went to plan in the first round as I exerted some educated pressure on him. I was on top of him throughout, doing all the right things. The second round continued in much the same vein and I went 5–3 up. After each round I stood in my corner while he sat down. I had decided that I would not sit down in the ring for the whole of the tournament, because I wanted to apply maximum psychological pressure on my opponents.

In the third I relaxed a bit, and he had a really good round which caught me on the hop. I hadn't seen too much to worry me, so I stupidly dropped my guard and relieved some of the pressure on him. I just switched off and had a really lazy round, and suddenly it was over and I was trailing as I went into the fourth and last. I was 8–6 down and Kelvin and Ian gave me a rocket in my corner. I said that all I needed was four left crosses and the fight would be over. This was not how I had planned it, but I knew I had the artillery in place if the cavalry charge was beaten back. I knew I could take him out with one big punch. And that's exactly what happened. I caught him with a beauty to the nose and mouth that left him wobbling like a screen drunk.

Earlier in the day the German Koc had been knocked out cold for five minutes by the Cuban Rublacaba just fifteen seconds into the fight. (I have to admit to feeling just a little pleased that day because both the guys I had lost to in the qualifiers would be out of the competition proper at the first hurdle.) But Koc's knockout meant the officials became even more paranoid about safety. On another day Lezin might have been allowed to continue, but it would have made no difference to the outcome because the man was now a quivering jelly who didn't know his arse from his elbow.

My delight at winning was clouded by a major injury worry. When I hit him with the left cross that ended the fight I immediately felt a stab of pain in my problem knuckle. It was ironic that the very punch which had rescued my Olympic dream had almost wrecked it at the same time. Once I had got my gloves off it quickly swelled up. 'This is serious,' I thought. But after I had kept it in ice for two days the swelling went right down and I was able to start hitting the pads in training again. I never thought the injury would rule me out there and then, but the problem was clearly going to be with me right through to the final if I got there. As I inspected the damage, Holyfield came up to me and said, 'You're a good guy, Audley, you're a good guy,' like I had just helped an old lady across the road.

My victory made some headlines back home because everyone had thought the Russian would be too strong for me. It was the same in the Olympic village, where some of the other athletes admitted that they hadn't thought I would make it. I was glad I had had such a tough first fight, because it primed me mentally for the challenges that lay ahead. If I had waltzed it I would have faced the danger of complacency, but that fight gave me a jolt and reminded me of the importance of getting in front early and then keeping up the pressure.

In the second-round fight I faced another eastern European fighter, Ukraine's Olekseii Mazikin, who had just beaten New Zealander Angus Shelford, nephew of All Black Wayne. I had never fought him before and knew nothing about him because he was a relatively new face on the scene. But I got hold of a video of his fight against Shelford and must have watched it about thirty times to analyse his style. He was as tall as me and obviously a tough, resilient fighter, but his reach wasn't that long and he was young and inexperienced.

I took a couple of rounds to get the measure of him and, leading 7–5 going into the third, I realised his slow hands and shorter arms were never going to cause me too much bother. In the last two rounds I was all over him and the crowd were loving it. I started showboating, turning it on for the Barmy Army who were in now full voice. (Kate Hoey, the then Sports Minister, was also there, although I think her support was a little more reserved. I feel she was a great ambassador for sport. She made a real difference and I do believe she should have kept her position). As I extended my lead I dropped my arms and started dancing a few jigs, and for the first time I heard the chant 'Audley, Audley' sung to the tune of the well-known football equivalent 'Olé, Olé'. The crowd were just brilliant, and I couldn't believe how much support I had in there. There were people running around with flags and all the neutrals started picking up on the Audley chant and joined in. In amateur boxing you rarely get a big contingent of fans coming to watch and any support you get generally comes from the other boxers and their families. This was the best atmosphere I have ever experienced and carried me along to the final bell, a 19–9 victory and the guarantee of a bronze medal (two bronzes are awarded in boxing). I was delighted to have won a medal, but as far as I was concerned it was still only half-time.

Afterwards 'Aussie' Joe Bugner called me 'a lazy bugger', which made me laugh, and all the British papers jumped on the comments – although to be fair to him he also said some very complimentary things about me. He said that, if I could get my jab going at full throttle and use my left hook more, there was no one in Sydney who could stand his ground against me. He thought my 'laziness' was the only threat to me taking the gold medal, but I refute the accusation that I am an idle boxer. The way I saw it, the fight was going to be won and lost on the putting greens, not on the first tee. My style is not about a blood-and-thunder work rate, piling in there like I'm in a pub car park at chucking out time on a Friday night. I am a thinking boxer, a tactical fighter. I wanted to land quality punches. If I end up in a brawl I'll look after myself, but I like to dictate the tempo of the fight and the tempo that I like as an amateur starts slowly and rises to a crescendo. Why rush in and open yourself up? Apart from anything else, a calm, studious approach often unsettles an opponent who wants to get it on.

In the semi-final I would be up against the Italian Paolo Vidoz, a solid, tough opponent who would carry on fighting even if you knocked his head off. I had beaten him in a European qualifier in Athens in December, but I was expecting it to be the toughest fight of my career. The hand was a worry because I had used it a few more times than I wanted to against Mazikin and it had flared up again. I knew I would need both hands to beat Vidoz, so I had a cortisone injection – that helped, but the hand was still a bit sore and swollen. Of all my international opponents during my amateur years he was probably the one I had the most respect for because of the brave way he fought and the dignified way he carried himself out of the ring. We didn't speak all that often, but we would always nod or smile when we saw each other at the weigh-in or around the arena. He was a thirty-year-old, as experienced as they come and, though he had slow feet, I couldn't let him get too close because he would have fun with me at close quarters. He likes to break people down slowly. I would have to keep him at arm's length and let my superior speed overwhelm him. I had seen him described in one paper as a 'cab rank' fighter (i.e. a pub scrapper), but this was a little unfair. He was not the most sophisticated fighter, but he was still a dangerous opponent who had twice finished third in the World Championships.

The entire arena was now dedicated to boxing and there was a full house of ten thousand as I walked out for the fight. The atmosphere was blinding and I had never experienced anything like it in the past. Some people get overwhelmed by big crowds, but I love an audience and as I strode into the ring I was lifted by the noise and the colour and felt invincible.

It was a ding-dong of a fight from the first bell. Just as I had expected, Vidoz threw himself at me and we were toe-to-toe for the whole two minutes, with both of us throwing a flurry of good punches. I was using my jab, and powering in some left crosses to devastating effect: by the end of the round I was leading 8–4 and he had a broken nose and was covered in blood. I stretched my lead by another two points in the second, but by the end of the third, which I lost 5–3, he had closed the deficit to three. But that was the closest he ever got. I had cut him under his eye and it was getting wider and wider with each punch, while his nose looked as if it had exploded. At the end of the third I sat down for the first time in the tournament. Neither of us had held anything back and I was seriously short of puff. But, barring a knockout, I knew a place in the final was mine. I looked over to Vidoz's corner and he looked like he had been in a car accident.

The break allowed me to recover my energies. I launched into him in the final round and unleashed the full repertoire of my skills, coming at him from all angles with every combination of blows. At one point I did a Sugar Ray Leonard windmill loop and caught him with a cracking upper cut. I won the round by a massive 15–2 and when I went 32–16 up, technically the fight should have been stopped (a new rule stated that a bout must be stopped if the gap is 15 points or more). In the end he had to take a standing count. He survived the round but my victory was never in doubt.

I look back on that fight as the best of my entire amateur career. In my first two fights I had been fairly cautious in my approach and narrowed my game. I fought within myself and approached my opponent in a scientific way. But against Vidoz I had decided to open up and show the world what I was really capable of. I wanted to put on an exhibition of all the weapons in my armoury and I had everything that day: heart, power and technique, as well as speed of hand, foot and thought. I totally took him to school. I fought him on the inside, I fought him on the outside. I brawled, I danced, I picked him off with a whole range of combinations. I was all over him, and by the end he was out on his feet.

The British fans, once again, were just unbelievable – the best by a mile of all the supporters there, even the Australians. Most people go through life without ever hearing their name being chanted – nor had I before Sydney – but it's one of the best sounds you will ever hear. Unfortunately, there were few other British athletes there to see the fight. In the first two rounds there were always plenty of tickets around, but for the semi and the final you couldn't get tickets for love or money. They were sell-outs. But the group of family and friends who had followed me out to Sydney was there in full cry. Hazel was there sitting right at the front of the arena, screaming and shouting until she was almost hoarse. Tony Burns was almost choking with excitement. Terry, my brother, had almost lost his voice by the end and when I was being interviewed for television straight after the fight I had to try and keep a straight face because I could see Akim and Wendl, who both worked at Repton, and a friend called Julian, jumping up and down like trampoliners. Rodney was capturing the moment on video, which has been replayed many times. It was pandemonium at ringside and I was grinning like a Cheshire Cat and waving the Union Jack. Courtney's mum, who says that I am her biggest idol after her son, could barely contain herself. She was trying to get past a security guard to come and congratulate me, so I shouted over to let her through and she came running over and gave me a big hug and a kiss.

Vidoz is a noble boxer and I appreciated his dignity in defeat. He said I deserved to be Olympic champion and that I never gave him a chance. He didn't make any excuses. To say these things when he must have been in a deep gloom just minutes after he had seen four years of hard work and dreams of Olympic glory being shattered is a great testament to his character. That's what I love about the Olympics and boxing at its best: even if you lose, the human spirit can still triumph. He wished me all the best in my future life – and good luck to him too. He is an honourable man and a credit to amateur boxing and his country.

Terry Edwards had remained in Sydney despite being effectively made redundant, but after my win over Vidoz he decided to return to England. Unsurprisingly, he never came to say goodbye before packing his bags. I had a silver medal in the bag and the gold was within my reach. In the final I would be up against the relatively unknown Mukhtarkhan Dildabekov of Kazakhstan. However, the biggest threat came not from him but from my own left hand, which was a mess. The cortisone injection, which works like an anaesthetic, had allowed me to punch freely against Vidoz, but after I had removed my gloves and the effect had worn off it was plain to see – and feel – that my knuckle could yet deny me gold. It had swollen up to the size of a golf ball and it was throbbing more than ever. It was so painful that I couldn't even make a proper fist. I wasn't worried about it in the fight itself, because after nine years leading up to this moment I was more than prepared to fight through eight minutes of agony. My fear was that the official doctor would stop me from fighting. The semi-final was on Friday and the final on Sunday, which gave me roughly two days to get the swelling down so that the doctor would pass me. On the first night I kept my left hand in a bucket of iced water until about one o'clock, but when I went to bed I still couldn't make a fist.

As I sat on my bed that night I punched my pillow with my good hand and shouted 'Fuck!' at the top of my voice. I honestly believed my Olympic dream was over. I had got to within one fight and eight minutes of the gold medal I had set my heart on four years earlier and it looked like I was going to be denied, not by another boxer, but by a knuckle. The difference between gold and silver was enormous – the same difference that separates the football Premier League winners from the runners-up. Going to Sydney wouldn't have been all for nothing, but if I was prevented from fighting the negative impact on my career plans would have been enormous. Somehow 'Audley Harrison, Olympic silver medallist' doesn't have quite the same ring about it.

I did not sleep well the night before the final. Fretting about my injury, I tossed and turned and dozed off only a bit. I went to bed at half past one and got up at five o'clock. My previous three fights had all been in the late evening and my body clock had become adjusted to a fairly set pattern, but because the final was about five hours earlier than these I got up at daybreak to make sure my natural rhythms weren't upset. I had breakfast with Stephanie Cook and Kate Allenby, the modern pentathletes who were also gunning for medals on the final day. They were eating muesli and bananas and I think they were a little surprised to see me tucking into a giant fry-up. Despite my worries about my hand, the three of us bantered away and geed each other for what lay ahead. There we sat, in a deserted dining hall at the start of the biggest days of our careers, buzzing with a heady mixture of excitement and nerves. By the time the sun set, we would all know whether we had achieved what we had been slowly working towards for so many years.

The weigh-in and the medical took place at eight o'clock, and when the time came for me to be inspected by the doctor he held my hands, looked into my eyes and asked me how I was feeling. I said, 'Perfect, thanks', but before he had a chance to inspect my knuckle he saw that I had a couple of days' growth of facial hair. In my rush to get to the pre-fight medical I had forgotten to shave. (In amateur boxing it is obligatory to have a shaved face. Beards are illegal.) I told him that I hadn't brought my shaving gear from the village and he got really worked up and sent me off to find a razor and some foam.

Cursing the Marquess of Queensberry, I rushed off in search of men's toiletries. It all seemed a bit ridiculous. There I was a few hours before the Olympic boxing super-heavyweight final wandering around the complex asking strangers if they happened to have a razor and some shaving foam I could quickly borrow. Finally, the medical centre was able to help. It turned out that I wasn't the first boxer in the tournament to have overlooked this crucial area of personal hygiene. When I returned to the doctor, my face as smooth as a boxing glove, he gave me a beaming smile and said, 'That's more like it, Mr Harrison.' And then he let me go, having completely forgotten to check out my hand. It was, if you'll excuse the expression, a very close shave indeed.

I spent the rest of the morning being given treatment on my

knuckle as well as physio on the rest of my body. The knuckle came down a little bit but the reduction was barely noticeable. Getting past the doctor had lifted my spirits for a while, but as the final grew ever closer I sank into a very black mood. I just lay there in the changing room stretched out on the bed with my headphones and shades on while all these people went to work on my body. I barely said a word in those final few hours as I sat there feeling extremely sorry for myself.

It is difficult to say what was bothering me – I had the normal pre-fight nerves and was also worried about my various injury problems. But although I wasn't aware of it at the time, I think the main difficulty was the great weight of the moment bearing down on me. I had arrived at the most critical point of my career. Ten years of hard battles to get here lay behind me, while two very different futures lay ahead. Which one of them would be mine depended entirely on what was about to happen in those eight minutes in the ring.

One bad day at the office and I would return to England with a pat on the back, a silver medal for the trophy cabinet and reasonable prospects of getting a professional contract that would give me financial stability. It would not be a bad life, but it wasn't the one I had had in mind in the years leading up to the Games. Win, and my life would be transformed forever. I would have done something no Briton had managed for over thirty years, when a man was yet to walk on the moon and before I had even been born. I would be an Olympic gold medallist. On top of that glory, money would never be a problem again and I would be in a position to give my family and friends a helping hand. I would be a household name and could virtually write my own cheque. The difference between a gold and a silver medal in financial terms could be as much as £50 million. I don't want to sound un-Corinthian, but I would be lying if I said I was in Sydney just for the taking part. If I lost, then of course I would have accepted my defeat with dignity and for the rest of my life I would feel proud that I had represented my country to the best of my abilities and come away with a silver medal to show for it. But I didn't set out on the Olympic trail to find silver at the end of it. Gold was the only goal.

With these thoughts swarming around in the back of my mind, I grew moodier and moodier as the telling moment drew ever closer. My knuckle was agony and I screamed when they put in the final cortisone injection. Outside my changing room there were thousands of fans crammed into the arena, and within minutes TV cameras would be beaming my image to every corner of the globe as I walked out to confront my boxing destiny. Just as we were preparing to leave the room and I was struggling to get myself into the zone I was handed a fax. It was from Lennox Lewis at his training camp in the Pocono Mountains in Pennsylvania, and read: 'We are all proud of the way you've been performing and you're doing yourself and your country proud.' It ended: 'From one Olympic champion to another – respect.' I barely knew Lennox at this time and had spoken to him properly just once when, at his party after beating the South African Frans Botha, he had taken me aside to give me some advice. I couldn't believe that he had gone to the trouble of sending me a good luck fax, timed so that I would read it just as I was about to walk out.

I had received hundreds of good luck faxes and e-mails from back home and had stuck all them on my wall in my room in the village. But this one was extra-special. I felt a shiver of goose pimples as I read it and then a great surge of aggression. I stuck the fax on the wall, kicked the cubicle door of the changing rooms off its hinges and marched into the corridor. I was pumped. I was going to win the gold whether it was with one fist or two. All the gloom that had been hanging over me like an electric storm that morning instantly lifted and I felt as light as a bantamweight as I skipped into the venue with the music pounding, Union Jacks everywhere and the fans shouting themselves daft.

As I approached the ring I saw some familiar faces in the ringside seats: my brothers Rodney and Terry, Hazel, Tony Burns, some friends from Repton and a couple of non-boxing mates from London. In the corner opposite me was a man I knew very little about. Dildabekov, a young soldier, had only recently established himself as Kazakhstan's number one super-heavyweight. Like all the members of his squad, he was in line for $100,000 if he won the gold – a small fortune for someone from the former Soviet republic.

He was not on my original list of most dangerous opponents but he was a World Championship silver medallist and, having beaten the Cuban Rubalcaba in the quarters and got to the Olympic final, I had to assume he was a serious threat. I had watched him a lot on video over the three days before the final and to me he seemed like a busy, fast boxer with a crude haymaker right hand, not especially stylish but a tough cookie.

As always I was fairly cautious in the first round, but I was purposeful and stalked him around the ring before rushing him at the end and forcing him to take a standing count. 'Square up, size up, beat up' was my game plan in Sydney. I finished the first 3–2 up and in the second I just went at him with everything I had, using both fists. In the heat of the moment, with the adrenalin rushing around my system, I almost forgot about the pain. I knew he didn't have the power to hurt me, but he kept chucking in these right-hand bombs over the top. So I got in close on him and started using upper cuts to good effect. When I had to pull back I hit him with some left crosses and by the end of the round I was in the clear, 9–4.

The third round was the best of the bout, an educated slugging match. At one point he closed the gap on me to just one point, but I hit back with a flurry of excellent combinations and as the round drew to a close the crowd went into a rendition of 'Audley, Audley'. The Kazak and I were punching our hearts out. At one point he caught me with two big punches in rapid succession but I just stayed there and, to the delight of the crowd, returned them with interest. It was a hell of a round and at the end of it, for only the second time in the Games, I sat down to take a breather. Dildabekov had given it everything he had in the third, and we both knew that it was now all over bar my showboating. He had thrown everything he could at me, but I had just thrown it back in his face.

The Kazak's spirit was broken. In the fourth round he was obviously even more tired than me, and in the opening exchanges I let him punch himself out. During his early swarm of punches he managed to tag me with a couple and then I launched myself at him for a final assault. I was now about ninety seconds away from realising my dream and I piled into him like his worst nightmare. The crowd were in full cry as I finished him off, willing me past the winning post, and then I heard the sweetest sound in the world, the final bell. It was 30–16 and I was an Olympic gold medallist.

I'd like to say that I was delirious with excitement in those first few minutes after the fight, but the truth is that I felt shattered, as if every last scrap of energy and every drop of sweat had been squeezed from my body. I was panting for breath. I had worked harder in my last two fights than in any other of my entire career, and my body just couldn't take me any further.

I looked out across the crowd, and amongst the waving Union Jacks I saw all the Turks, Germans and French who just a few months earlier had been slagging me off in Belgium as no more than a gym fighter. It was a lovely sight. These three teams, with about twenty-five boxers in total, had won just one gold and two bronzes between them and there I was, now the Olympic gold medallist and a name to mention in the same breath as Ali, Frazier, Spinks, Lewis, Foreman and De La Hoya. And no one, not even my fiercest critics, could say that I didn't deserve it. I had won my victories in the semi-final and final by landslides and had exhibited a full repertoire of boxing skills. I didn't say anything to these guys who had been laughing at me in Belgium because I didn't need to. My actions had drowned out their words.

Holding a Union Jack, I walked to each side of the ring and saluted the crowd. The British fans had been magnificent and they were the first people I wanted to thank. Then I walked over to the officials and looked them all straight in the eye and smiled. I had nothing against these particular officials, but they knew what I was smiling about. There are rumours about corruption in amateur boxing so I wanted to remind everyone that I had come the whole distance and won the gold medal fair and square. Afterwards several of the referees from the Commonwealth and from African countries came up and congratulated me and asked to have their photographs taken with me – but not one of the Europeans from the Eastern Bloc, approached me.

I was mobbed by TV crews as I walked out of the ring and headed backstage to freshen up before the medal ceremony. When I used to dream about standing on that podium, with 'God Save the Queen' booming out of the speakers, I was always very emotional, but when it came to the real thing I was still too hyped and too tired to feel much. You always hear athletes on the TV saying, 'Well, it hasn't really sunk in yet' and it sounds like a cliché, but that's exactly how I felt when the medal was put around my neck. There were no tears and I almost felt numb. I barely had time to take the whole thing in. I was rushed along through well-wishers and media, I climbed on to the podium, the National Anthem was played, the flag was raised, I acknowledged the crowd and then I walked off. I had a passing sense of having reached the top of my Mount Everest, but not for a couple of hours did the magnitude of my achievement fully strike home. Someone told me in the mêlée that my breakfast companions Stephanie Cook and Kate Allenby had also won medals, gold and bronze respectively, in the modern pentathlon. Weirdly, I felt an even bigger lift for them than I had done for myself. I couldn't relate to my own reality. It was almost as if I needed to step outside of myself and look back in order to appreciate what I had achieved. But in the emotional and physical chaos that followed my victory, I was far too unsettled to be able to do that.

At the press conference I picked up the microphone as all the journalists filed in and I did a little rap song to remind them that they had never given me a chance and I had proved them wrong. It was all good-natured stuff and everyone was laughing. This was my honeymoon period, and I was enjoying the irony of it as dozens of the hacks asked me to autograph their accreditation cards. In a few months, I knew, many of these guys would be sharpening their knives as I embarked on my professional career. I felt a great sense of satisfaction as I surveyed the press corps assembled before me now, hanging on my every word and falling over themselves to ask me questions. It was true that I had talked a great fight, but most of the journalists had believed that that was all I could do. But did they really think that I was deluding myself all that time? That I was prepared to risk humiliation by saying I was going to win and then perform like Eddie the Eagle? If I had thought I only had an outside chance of a gold, I would have said exactly that. But I genuinely believed I had a real chance of going the whole way and I wouldn't have put my head on the block if I didn't. I am not stupid and I am a proud man. There is no way I would have risked humiliating myself by overstating my chances, only to get flattened. There was, of course, always the chance that I might get caught out by a stray haymaker, but as I said when I quoted the French dramatist Pierre Corneille at that press conference: 'Triumph without risk is triumph without glory.' Walk the walk and talk the talk. I had delivered on my word and these journalists were forced to respect me whether they liked it or not. What better answer could I have given?

I had won Britain's first Olympic boxing gold for thirty-two years and the first in the top weight division since Ronald Rawson in 1920. Mine was only Britain's fourth boxing gold since 1924, and followed Finnegan's in Mexico and those won by Dick McTaggert and Terry Spinks in Melbourne in 1956. (The parallels with Finnegan were uncanny: he too struggled to qualify and was close to having to pull out of the final because his hand was so swollen.)

I could have stayed in Darling Harbour forever to celebrate my greatest victory, but we had to head back to the village in order to get ready for the closing ceremony later that evening. It was then, as I walked down the hill from the main gate towards the apartments in the GB camp, still buzzing from the final, that I walked straight into the rest of Team GB and was mobbed by my cheering team-mates. Not once in the nine years since I had taken up boxing had I allowed myself to feel a sense of satisfaction. I was always yearning for something more and as soon as I had met one challenge I just moved on to the next. There was no respite – until that moment in the village in Sydney when all the urgency and tension just fell away as my friends in the British team smothered me in congratulations. I had realised my dream.

As we headed off to the Olympic Stadium, the atmosphere amongst the GB team was unbelievable. Everyone was singing and taking photographs and jumping on each other's backs. We were like a group of good-natured football fans whose team had just won the Cup. Before they led us through to the stadium, we were put into a holding area where I saw Stephanie and Kate and we all gave each other a big hug. It seemed like three weeks ago, not twelve hours, that we had sat down at breakfast bleary-eyed and a little tense before our final performances. As we walked through the long tunnel into the stadium the mood became even more boisterous and some of the athletes, including Matthew Pinsent, Tim Foster and myself, climbed up a ladder and started waving the Union Jack while the rest of the team chanted songs. Inside it was party time, and we were all shepherded on to the grass in the middle of the track.

We must have been there for an hour or so when Courtney and I realised we were running late to meet our friends and family, whom we had arranged to see in a Chinese restaurant. But the officials wouldn't let us back across the track for love or money – we were trapped. In the end we just pushed one of the stewards out of the way and sprinted out of the arena like a pair of naughty schoolboys. We ran straight into an oncoming crowd of athletes, performers and officials, and could barely move as we tried to push our way out to the street. Finally a policeman put us into the back of a car and drove us to the village, where we slid into some casual clothes and then ran to the restaurant where everyone greeted us with a huge cheer.

The celebrations that night were never going to live up to what had happened after the Commonwealths, but I still had one of the best nights of my life. At dinner everyone got up in turn to propose a toast to me, and we drank the place out of champagne before heading off to a club called the Cave. As the night wore on the club filled up with hundreds of athletes from different countries. It was a cattle market for thoroughbreds and, not being funny, I was spoilt for choice on the lady front. Not once all evening did I go and chat up a girl. I just stood there and they came to me. There were a couple of girls whom I had got a bit cheeky with over the last few weeks, but I hadn't got involved because I didn't want to be distracted from my medal quest. I had said, 'Well, let's wait until after the Games and we'll see what happens.' They were both there in the club that night, and each of them came up to me and suggested we went back to the village. But I said no in each case. I was out celebrating my gold medal with the rest of the athletes, my family and friends, and I didn't want to be slipping away no matter how attractive the offers and no matter how pleasurable the experience might have been. Love could wait ... but only just. An American model started hitting on me in the last couple of hours and it took every last grain of willpower in my body to keep myself in the club. We danced and drank until about four o'clock before I dropped her at the Holiday Inn, where she was staying, and I returned to the village (by myself) and grabbed an hour's bad sleep before getting up to pack and heading to the airport for the flight home. Honest.

As the plane took off from Sydney I was finally able to reflect on the previous seven weeks as well as on the nine years' hard graft that had finished, as I had intended, with me stepping on to the podium to have the Olympic gold medal placed around my neck.

To be part of Britain's best performance at the Olympics for seventy-six years made me feel very proud. We had won twenty-eight medals in all, including eleven golds. Four years earlier we had finished thirty-sixth, behind Ethiopia, Algeria and North Korea, but this time the team would be returning to a heroes' welcome and it would be my face dominating the front page of most newspapers back home. Denise Lewis and Steve Redgrave had had their moments of glory, and because my final was almost the last event of the Games I was the big news story of the moment along with Stephanie Cook.

I like to think that my triumph has provided amateur

boxing in Britain with a great shot in the arm. Before Sydney, the average sports fan would hardly have known that amateur boxing existed. I hope that the sport can build on my victory and that even more funding will be made available and more youngsters will take up the sport. That gold medal was as much for the future of British amateur boxing as it was for me. The kids have got to dream, just as I did. With any luck they will find a better system in place to help them, too. After Terry Spinks won gold in Melbourne in 1956 he returned to a hero's welcome and rode a white horse through the East End. I doubted I would be doing the same through the streets of Wembley and Harlesden, but at least amateur boxing would be back on the map.

Another heartening aspect of the Olympics was that the boxing was one of the 'cleanest' tournaments I can remember participating in. There were virtually no rumours of dodgy deals or officials – just a bit of petty cheating. For instance, boxers were not allowed to know the score during their bouts, but several trainers had been kept informed on the mobile phone by people who were watching the fights back stage, on television.

I got a taste of what was in store for me back in England when we stopped over in Singapore. Total strangers started coming up and asking for my autograph. Television crews followed me around in the transit lounge as we waited for the plane to be refuelled. One of the photographers took a picture of Denise and me which ended up in the *Sun* the following day, starting rumours about us as an item. I have to admit that it would have been a great story for the papers to wrap up the Games – 'Gold medallists Lewis and Harrison in love!' – but I'm afraid there was no truth in the speculation.

It was only when we arrived back at Heathrow after a twenty-hour journey that I understood the full scale of the media and public interest. It was simply phenomenal. We knew that there had been great support for Team GB back home over the previous three weeks, but when you are 12,000 miles way it is very difficult to feel it. You are aware of it, but you don't experience it – you can't touch it. Then, at the moment we walked through passport control and customs, it hit us like a wall. There were camera bulbs flashing and TV crews and journalists swarming over us like the plague. 'Audley, can I have a quick word? . . . Audley, how does it feel? . . . Audley, what are your plans now. . . ?' I went into full marketing spiel as I walked along the line of reporters. I had done the boxing, now it was time to milk the exposure. There was an official press conference for all the medallists and Simon Clegg asked me to sit in the centre and be the official spokesman. I thought that was a nice touch. (During the conference one of the photographers called me Audrey by mistake. Everyone went dead quiet for a moment before the place collapsed as I climbed over the table and pretended I was going to sort him out.)

When I had left London seven weeks earlier, I walked around the airport and no one recognised me. The only people outside my family and circle of friends who knew who I was were the rest of the team, some journalists and other amateur boxers. I could go into W.H. Smith's at the airport, buy a newspaper and the girl at the checkout would say, 'That'll be 30p please, sir,' without even looking up. Seven weeks later, when we arrived back, the girl stared at me like I was a ghost. 'You're Audley Harrison,' she stammered nervously (like I didn't know). Everywhere people stared and pointed, heads turned, and everyone from old grannies to kids asked me to sign autographs, handing me scraps of paper, newspapers, cigarette packets – anything – to sign. It is one of the ironies of fame: wealth gives you freedom, but the limelight restricts it.

Celebrity, I was quickly discovering, was great, but it was going to be a huge pressure. You have to be all things to all people, you have to be on your guard at all times and you have to be unfailingly patient, graceful and grateful. There might be fifty schoolboys screaming and jostling at your feet, stuffing pieces of paper in your face to sign while in the background photographers snap away, the television cameraman is prowling, the microphone boom is hovering overhead and journalists are hanging around with their notepads – and all you want to do sometimes is slip away and have a quiet evening at home or out with some friends. But you can't. With celebrity comes responsibility. You can't be grumpy, you can't be impatient, you can't be short with people. No matter how much you try to control your own life, you have to accept that you have become public property, part of other people's lives.

The public had invested their admiration and respect in me, and they had cheered me when I won gold. I had made my fans feel good about themselves when I represented Britain and saw off the world's all-comers in Sydney. They felt that they shared in my triumph in some way, and I was acutely aware of this the day we landed at Heathrow. Only Steve Redgrave, and possibly Denise Lewis, received more attention than me when we got back to England. I wasn't surprised to find people interested in me, but the intensity of that interest took my breath away.

Everyone wanted a slice of me – but I wanted a slice of me more than anyone else. The only time I had had to myself in the last few weeks was when I had crawled into bed and turned the light off. I felt like I had been at the centre of a big crowd for a month, with dozens of different voices firing questions at me or offering me advice. My life had been changed forever, my world turned on its head in just a few weeks. I used to be 'Audley Harrison, man in the street', now I was 'Audley Harrison, Olympic champion, please form an orderly queue'. I enjoyed the attention, was flattered by the adulation, respect and warmth of people towards me, and knew it wasn't going to go away, probably ever.

My Dad drove me from the airport, but we headed for his house because someone had called him and told him the press were waiting outside mine. When we got to Pinner he took me into all his local shops pretending he had to do some shopping, but all he was doing was showing me off. He was like an excited little kid as we went into the bakery, then the estate agent and the greengrocer's. In his local newsagent he picked up one of the papers with a picture of me on the front and pointed out to anyone coming into the shop who wanted to listen that that was me, his son. He was really proud. As he was parading me around, I couldn't help but think back to that time when I was a runaway teenager and he and my brothers pinned me down in the back of the car and told me to get my life together. We went to drop off my half-brother Adam at school, and once again Dad made me get out of the car. Adam's mates were all buzzing around me at the school gates asking to have a look at my gold medal, so I took it out of my pocket and let them touch it. They seemed just like me about fifteen years earlier and passed the medal, around as if it was the secret to everlasting life, gasping and going 'Wow!'

In the car on the way home (a few hours later than I had intended) Dad told me that he had watched the whole of the final even though he had had no absolutely no intention of doing so. He had never watched a whole fight of mine before because he gets so nervous. For my first three fights in Sydney he was upstairs with his head buried in his bedclothes until the fight was over. Only then would he come downstairs and turn on the telly to see if I had won. But the final was delayed by about ten minutes – roughly the length of the fight if it went the distance. So when he came downstairs expecting the fight to be over it was just being introduced. He had no choice but to watch it. He said he had never been so nervous in all his life as he was during those eight minutes, and when I won he cried his eyes out.

After arriving back in London that morning my life became one long, crazy roller-coaster – and I have been loving every minute of it. Some serious business lay ahead, but for the first few weeks I was going to do nothing but relax and learn how to enjoy myself again. A boxer's life is a pretty Spartan one. You can't go out in the evening, you can't eat whatever you want, you can't drink alcohol, you get up at the crack of dawn, you run up hills, you pull cars and you spar. It's not exactly a life of leisure – more like the regime of a prisoner of war. Over the coming months I would have to undergo an operation on my knuckle and then I would have to start assembling a team for my professional career. I would need a good lawyer, manager, trainer, promoter and television network, and there would be all sorts of business and sponsorship deals to sort out. But for the moment that could wait.

I hadn't been to many parties or functions over the last year, but by Christmas I was starting to feel like Tara Palmer-Tompkinson. On my birthday, 26 October, I threw a huge party in Browns in the West End. At the last party I had thrown only my family and my mates were there. This time they were all there again, but the joint was also crawling with celebrities: Jordan, people from *EastEnders*, premiership footballers, Precious, top British boxers and other athletes from the Olympics. It was absolutely heaving and by one o'clock the door were operating a policy of one in, one out. Two weeks earlier I had been to the last-ever football match at Wembley with Denise Lewis and Steve Redgrave. England lost to Germany, which was depressing, but at half-time the three of us were given an unbelievable reception by the fans when we were walked out to the centre of the pitch. It was a bad day for

England and the weather was horrible, but I will always have good memories of it.

There were also a number of formal receptions for the Olympic squad, including one with the Queen where all the gold medallists were introduced to her. Princess Anne took me over to her, saying, 'Mummy, this is the boxer Audley Harrison I was telling you about.'

The Queen said, 'Of course, I know all about you.' (A few days earlier the *Sun* had splashed the news of my wild past and my imprisonment across the front page and this flashed through my mind as she smiled at me. 'I bet you do,' I thought.) The Queen was really pleasant and told me how proud I should feel after what I had achieved.

There was also a reception in the Science Museum in South Kensington, where we were introduced to Tony and Cherie Blair. During those first few weeks back in England it felt as if my world had been turned completely upside down. Before going to Sydney the closest I had got to the Queen was licking the back of a first-class stamp; now I was shaking her hand and passing the time of day with her. It was all very weird.

I enjoyed my time basking in the warm glow of the British public's adoration. I knew (and still know) that it wasn't going to last, and that the knives were probably already being sharpened in Fleet Street. There is always a risk of over-exposure, of people getting bored of you. They see you on telly and hear you on the radio, they see your pictures in papers and mags and naturally they will begin to tire of you as other people move into the limelight and elbow you to one side. It happens to most people in the public eye, and only a few have managed to stay popular throughout their career. But I'm going to enjoy it while it lasts, and in a way I'm starting all over again. A new stage of my life is beginning. I'm at the bottom of a new, even higher mountain, the Everest of professional boxing, and it's going to be a tough climb with a lot of hardship if I'm ever going to get to the top and plant my flag. I am more aware than anyone how difficult it will be to become world champion, but I am determined to do it and I honestly believe that, barring accident or injury, I can do it. I've got all the tools. I told everyone I was going to be national champion, then Commonwealth champion. No one believed me. I told everyone I was going to be Olympic champion. People laughed. Now I am saying that I am going to have a tilt at becoming world champion.

One thing is for sure: it's not going to happen overnight. It's going to take a lot of sweaty dedication and bloody determination. After winning Olympic gold it took Floyd Patterson four years and thirty-two fights, Ali four years and twenty fights, Frazier six years and twenty-five fights, Foreman five years and thirty-eight fights and Lewis five years and twenty-three fights.

I had barely showered off the sweat from the final when the advice from people within the boxing world began to flood in. Within hours of the final bell greats like Sugar Ray Leonard, Evander Holyfield and Lennox Lewis had all told reporters how I should go about my life from now on. Flattery poured from the mouths of potential promoters and managers about how well I boxed, how smart I was, how I had the potential to be a great world champion, how dedicated I was to suffer all the financial hardships, that I was the future of British boxing, the hottest property in British sport overnight, that I was already big box-office on both sides of the Atlantic, the best thing since sliced bread, the only hope for peace in the Middle East, the man to cure the hole in the ozone layer and find a cure for cancer. . . .

I'm sure most of the praise I received was genuinely well meant, especially from the British guys who were delighted to see the country's boxing profile lifted by my success. But I wasn't born yesterday, either. The game had already begun.

The queue to sign me up was growing by the minute. I was being wooed and courted at long distance and it was difficult to distinguish the heartfelt congratulations from the attempts at seduction. I knew this was going to happen, and I knew I was going to have to be careful. It is easy to be flattered by someone's personal charm and their apparent high regard for you, especially if they start a conversation by saying, 'Audley, I could earn you £100 million in five years.'

# CHAPTER 10

# AT THE BOTTOM OF A NEW EVEREST

It was time to start punching for pay. I had no ready-made plan about how to start my professional career when I got back from Sydney, but I knew that a false move at the beginning could send me down the short road to the packed graveyard of failed professional boxers. I had just turned twenty-nine and by my reckoning I had about six, possibly seven years, left in the ring. If everything was managed right I would get a shot at the top titles as well as give myself financial security for life. I don't want to be still climbing into the ring when I am forty.

Most British boxers turn pro in their early twenties, partly because of the poor amateur scene, and more often than not they fail to make an impression because they are too inexperienced. Heavyweights tend to mature later than lighter boxers, who go downhill quickly once they have lost the speed and agility of their youth. At twenty-nine I felt I had the experience and maturity to make an impression in the professional ring at a time when I would be coming into my physical prime as a heavyweight.

The only worry at this stage was the knuckle injury which had caused me so much grief in Sydney, and which would require surgery before I could box again. The swelling was still the size of an egg on my return, but I had been put in contact with a leading surgeon in New York and, if the operation in November went well, I could expect to be back in the ring by March or April. In December I was called upon to add my voice to the row over the so-called barbarism of boxing after featherweight Paul Ingle fell into a coma following a fight in Sheffield. All the predictable calls to ban boxing were aired and an MP called Paul Flynn said he wanted to put a Bill through Parliament which would have boxers charged with assault or manslaughter if opponents were seriously injured or killed in the ring. Have you ever heard such rubbish? Plenty of others from all walks of life came out of the woodwork to call the sport barbaric and insisting it must be banned.

For me, the odds of being killed in the ring are the same as if I take a flight. Every now and then one is going to crash. It is a fact of modern life. So do we ban air travel? Someone, somewhere in the world will collapse in the ring from time to time, just as someone will fall off a horse, die on a mountain or get killed behind the wheel of a car. As far as I'm concerned it is not the remit of the politician or the medic to start imposing their moral judgements on the activities of others. To box or not to box is the decision for the individual, not society as represented by government or Mr Paul Flynn, MP for Newport West. We live in a society where individuals are allowed to exercise their own free will. This is not Stalinist Russia. Does Mr Flynn think boxers are so stupid they cannot weigh up their own balance of risks? Flynn said he did not want to ban boxing, only ban blows to the head. And while you're about it, Mr Flynn, why not take the jumps out of show jumping, the cars out of Formula One, the scrums out of rugby and the horses out of racing?

The lay-off did at least give me the time to give my full attention to the big decisions I would have to make in launching my professional career. I needed to put my team together. All my sponsorship deals had also come to an end so they would need renegotiating. Commercially, I was a free man and with an Olympic gold medal in my pocket I had a very powerful bargaining tool. I wanted total control over my career to avoid the exploitation that so many other boxers have suffered at the hands of greedy and unscrupulous promoters down the years. I am the first to admit that I am a control freak, but I see nothing wrong with wanting to be in charge of my own destiny, to make my own decisions. I have worked very hard to get where I am and I'm not going to throw it all away now. There are more poor ex-boxers than rich ones, despite the huge sums of money swilling around at the top end of the game.

I wanted a team of strong individuals with the emphasis on the team. When I stepped into the ring, I would be on my own. None of them would be able to help me. But I would only be in the ring for a maximum of twenty minutes a time, once every two months. The rest of the work would take place outside the ring, and there was plenty of work to be done.

I wanted people I could trust and I wanted the team to be a manageable size. What I didn't want was a huge entourage of hangers-on and a dodgy promoter with a gift for burying the killer clauses in the small print of contracts. Until recently a young, talented boxer would be plucked from the ring by a ruthless promoter, exploited for every penny and then just dumped when he was no longer considered box-office material. Nowadays, it is more and more the boxer who sets the agenda. Certainly, the best British boxers are the ones in control: Naseem Hamed and Lennox Lewis have both shown that they are not prepared to be sidelined in the important decision-making processes. It is amazing to think that for so many years the boxer, the one with the talent and the financial pulling power, has let the men-in-suits toy with his life. This was never going to happen with me. My experience of dealing with the amateur authorities had taught me nothing if not the importance of letting them know that it was me, the boxer, who was the central figure.

Everything had gone to plan so far: winning the ABA national title, the Commonwealths and then the Olympics. Now I had to make sure the next stage was just as well handled. The manager would have to be someone I could trust and who could find me the right opponents; the trainer would have to be able to condition me as a pro and improve my technique; the promoter would need to put on the best show in town; and the TV deal would have to give me the best coverage and the greatest exposure. I couldn't afford to make an error of judgement with any of these decisions, and I knew that offers would come at me from all directions. I would be wined and dined and flattered and generally made a fuss over; sums of money unimaginable just a few months earlier would be placed on the table before me; while all the time I would be swept along in the post-Olympics media frenzy. It was vital that I kept a cool head and did not let my judgement become disorientated amid all the hype and in the rush that some people would have me make towards a professional career. I had never been bossed around or manipulated in my life, even as a kid, and I didn't intend to start now.

The image of professional heavyweight boxing has suffered in recent years. The sport has become a bit of a circus in which a lot of promoters have feathered their own nests while short-changing the public. I wanted to give value for money, but the challenge for me in my first few fights was to provide good entertainment without getting over-ambitious. It was going to be a difficult tightrope to walk at first because it would be foolish to commit myself to fighting the top guys just a few months after taking off my amateur helmet and stepping into the professional arena. The gulf between amateur and professional boxing is immense, as wide as that between netball and NBA basketball. The last thing I wanted to do was get humiliated in my first couple of fights and derail my career barely before it had started. I could train for a year as a professional but the true tests come only in the ring, and I would need to get as much experience as possible before I could start challenging for the top honours.

I had barely put the key in the front door of my flat in Kingsbury after getting back from Sydney when the phone started to ring with offers from promoters and TV networks, both British and American. But I was in no rush. I just sat back, fielded the calls, said I would listen to all good offers and would get back to them in due course. I wanted to let the interested parties do all the talking at first so that I could get an idea of the sums of money involved and a feel for negotiating deals of this size. I knew a fair amount about business management from my studies, but I had every reason – and plenty of time – to be cautious. I didn't want to negotiate myself into a corner by declaring, 'I want £5 million for this', only to discover that their offer was actually going to be five times that. Also, the longer I held back and declined to commit myself, the more opportunity it gave to rival organisations to become involved – and once there were several players on the park I could play them off against each other.

There were only two people I needed to get on board quickly: a lawyer and someone to look after the money. The accountant bit was easy – I just called Hazel. She had been in the same job for seventeen years and after a brief spell in a new office, she came on board with me. I wanted all the accounts to be completely up-to-date and transparent from top to bottom, down to the last box of paper clips. Hazel oversees everything in the office. The search for a top lawyer who knew the world of boxing would be more difficult, but only slightly so.

Some of the best advice I received in those months came from Lennox Lewis, whom I spoke with at length after watching him defend his world title against the New Zealander David Tua in Las Vegas in November. Lennox told me to forget about America, where there was always the danger of becoming just another heavyweight boxer, and stay in Britain where I was already a household name. He said I could always come to the States for training sessions and spar against some of the best heavyweights around. He also stressed the importance of having a high-calibre legal team on board to make sure that every contract is thoroughly negotiated, detailed and watertight. The slip of a lawyer's pen can cost millions at this level.

I had met plenty of lawyers in the past, but most of those meetings had taken place in prison cells. Criminal lawyers weren't going to be much use to me now. I needed a leading civil lawyer who knew his boxing as well as his contract law. How I ended up with my lawyers is something of a mystery. I received a message on my answering machine from a journalist who didn't leave his name, recommending a barrister called Jonathan Crystal and a solicitor called Robert Davis, who handled several sports stars. Weirdly, the tip-off came at exactly the moment when I was giving all my attention to putting together the legal side of my affairs. I had nothing to lose by following up the recommendation, and so Hazel and I went to meet them shortly afterwards. We were instantly impressed by their knowledge of the professional boxing world and especially of the way it related to contract law. My mind was made up there and then.

Lennox had cemented his control over his own affairs when he set up Lennox Lewis Enterprises, with himself as president, and made his long-serving manager Frank Maloney and his promoter Panos Eliades directly answerable to him. It is well known in the boxing world that Lewis's steady rise in the boxing world and his accumulation of wealth have been very shrewdly managed by himself and the people around him. Outside the ring, professional boxing is like a chess game, and it is all too easy for boxers just to remain pawns on the board, small fry for the bigger pieces on the board to sacrifice at will.

My close contact with Lennox at this time led many people to believe that I would be hitching myself to his bandwagon, and I even saw one report stating that my first professional fight would be on his card. It is true that we had a lot in common: we were both super-heavyweights who had fought first at the Commonwealths, then at the Olympics. We are both Britons with links to other countries (me Jamaica, him Canada). I was now following him down the professional path and I hoped to become the heavyweight champion of the world. But that is the limit of our professional connection.

I have always admired Lewis as a boxer and was really touched by his good luck fax to me in Sydney. He's one of life's genuine good guys. He manages to get the right balance between humility and self-confidence. Around this time I was described in one paper as a heavyweight with the talent of Lewis and the appeal of Bruno. I can live with that. Lewis has proved himself to be a boxer of the highest calibre, a worthy world champion, truly the best around at the time. But although he is popular, he has never completely won the hearts of the British people as Bruno did. If he didn't have that mid-Atlantic accent and sounded a little more like Henry Cooper, I guess that wouldn't have been a problem.

With a good legal team at my side I was now in a position to start negotiating a television deal. There had been plenty of overtures from the top promoters on both sides of the Atlantic before, during and in the immediate aftermath of the Olympics. There had also been that one hard-and-fast offer from Frank Warren a couple of years earlier. But the first major player to emerge from the crowd – which is literally what he did – was Greg Dyke, the Director General of the BBC, who approached me at the England v Germany game at Wembley and said he would be very interested in us 'working together'. Sky had already made a tentative opening gambit, and so within a few days of returning to London I had two of the three big British players on the end of the phone talking telephone number sums of cash. ITV would also join the race, but they were slow out of the blocks and would retire early.

Under normal circumstances, a boxer finds a promoter and lets him sort out the deal with the television company. But these 'normal circumstances' didn't always produce the best possible deal for the boxer himself, so I decided to deal direct with the television networks. I would need a promoter at some point, but I saw no reason why I couldn't negotiate my own deal. After all, it was my career, my image, my personality and my life that were sitting in the middle of the negotiating table. If a promoter came to me with a great offer I was prepared to listen. He couldn't make me sign anything, and with my lawyers combing the details of any offer, I couldn't lose.

Which is where the two Franks come in – Warren and Maloney, the new double act of British boxing. The pair of them had been lavishing praise on me since Sydney, courting me through the media and in person. Throughout the next few months of negotiations, Warren would be on the phone to me at regular intervals. He was very much in the Sky camp, but he had enough contacts, clout and canniness to swing other deals as well. It wasn't just a straight case of join Warren and join Sky. Panos Eliades, Lennox Lewis' promoter, and Jonathan Feld and Ben Stone of the World Sports Organisation also made contact. Within a few weeks several big American promoters, including Don King, had introduced themselves. God knows how these people get hold of your personal telephone numbers, but I would be walking down the street or sitting having my breakfast when my mobile would ring and it would be someone from New York or Detroit or Vegas, making a sales pitch.

Don King never called me directly, but he told reporters he could earn me ten times more money than any other promoter, adding, 'The man does not need to go to the mountain, the mountain can come to him.' (You've got to admire the man's style.) But his people were in touch from the outset. This is how my first conversation with his 'people' went.

Girl on phone: 'Hi, Audley, I'm just ringing to say we've sorted you out tickets for the Tyson fight in Detroit and you'll be staying in the Hilton and someone will be picking you up from the airport on the Friday. We're all really looking forward to meeting.'

Me: 'That's very kind of you, but who the hell are you?'

Girl on phone: 'I'm in the boxing world, and I'm going to introduce you to all the right people when you come out here, Audley.'

Me: 'But who do you represent?'

Girl on phone: 'I represent a lot of the top people in professional boxing, Audley, and I'm on friendly terms with all the right people who can guide you in your career. It'll be real good for you out here, Audley. We'll make sure you are real well looked after.'

Me: 'So I have no idea who you are, but you want me to fly out to Detroit to meet you?'

Girl on phone: 'Hey, Audley, don't be like that. We just want the best for you. It's not going to cost you any money and, as I say, you'll meet all the big guys.'

Me: 'Who do you work for?

Girl on phone: 'Mr King is a brilliant man, Audley, and you shouldn't believe everything you read about him.'

Me: 'Well, if Mr King wants to work with me then Mr King

can make direct contact. We can meet face-to-face, but I'm not coming out to hover around in the shadows before possibly being granted an audience with the man.'

Girl on phone: 'Well, Audley, of course you will be meeting Mr King at some point, and of course you will get the chance to meet him face-to-face.'

Me: 'I've got to go. Goodbye.'

The circus grew by the day. Some of the acts in it were very impressive, but there were also a lot of clowns, some boxer-eating lions to be avoided at all costs, dwarves too small to bother about, and some tightrope walkers who looked exciting but were only ever a wobble away from crashing. Then there was me, just sitting in the crowd and enjoying the show as all the acts went through their familiar routines.

There were a number of options open to me at the beginning, but once I had decided that I wanted to stay in Britain the basic dilemma was this: Sky had the cash while the BBC had the audience. Which of those two I would go with was completely up in the air for the entire three or four months of these negotiations and even when matters rushed to a head early in 2001 I was still undecided.

By the New Year the race between the three networks to sign me was accelerating towards a conclusion. We had had meetings with all the head honchos, including Greg Dyke, Peter Salmon, Dominic Coles and Mike Lewis at the BBC and Vic Wakeling and his team at Sky. The whole process works like a seduction: it begins with mutual attraction, you eye each other up, then the phone rings and you chat and work out whether you are both interested, you go on your first date for dinner or lunch and they start coming on to you, then as you get more intimate they get a bit more nervous because they are close and they are thinking the time is right to make their move. I was playing the field with all three, but once it got down to the dirty business of hard money and sordid details

ITV got squeamish and pulled out of negotiations. One of the reasons why ITV dropped out was because they could not commit to resurrecting a midweek fight night programme, which the BBC were keen to do.

The BBC saw me as the perfect man to spearhead their campaign. The last live BBC fight had been broadcast in 1994, when Bruno beat Jesse Ferguson in the first round in an embarrassing mismatch. ITV's boxing coverage had also ended around then, as Warren took Bruno, Hamed and Nigel Benn to Sky. There has always been a massive boxing following in Britain, but it tailed off with the arrival of satellite TV and even more so with the introduction of pay-per-view. Most of the biggest audiences for sports events in the early 1990s were for boxing, and 18 million tuned in to watch Nigel Benn's famous but tragic victory over Gerald McClellan which left the American suffering long-term health problems.

Boxing used to be a permanent fixture on both networks and the sport enjoyed a very high profile. Until it was taken off terrestrial television most people with a passing interest in sport could probably reel off the names of a dozen top British boxers. But if you stopped a guy in the street today and asked him to name all the current British boxers he knew he would probably say Lennox Lewis and Naseem Hamed and, since the Olympics, probably Audley Harrison. The lack of exposure of professional boxing (not to mention amateur) has had terrible consequences for the profile of the sport. Terrestrial TV made them stars and kept boxing right up there with football and the other most popular sports. Sky have invested a lot in boxing and some of their coverage has been great, but the audience figures have dwindled and the pay-per-view fights have been a disaster. Boxing has become marginalised.

I was told that Dyke was keen to restore the BBC's interest in boxing and also that he wanted to groom me as a presenter on sports and lifestyle programmes. Dyke is a great fight fan and began his career in journalism as a freelance reporter covering amateur boxing in Hayes Town Hall for the then London *Evening News*. After meeting him at Wembley he introduced me to Peter Salmon, the new Director of Sport, who took over the negotiations. I was impressed with the whole package they were laying out and the detailed plans they had, not just for my fight career but also for my life after boxing. The BBC deal would bring boxing back into the homes of the wider public. If I went for Sky I would be on a sideshow for specialists, preaching to the converted as it were. Part of my mission as a boxer is to help restore boxing's fortunes, not just make my own fortune.

When I got back to England I read articles quoting top boxing people saying that I could earn as much as £60 million. After I won in Sydney, Evander Holyfield told the TV cameras I could expect to earn £150 million. Now that is serious money. But for me it has never been simply a case of cash. If it was, I would have taken the money of earlier offers and run. I knew that if I was a successful pro boxer I would make more money than most people could only dream of. In a way there is little difference between £10 million or £60 million because both sums of money would transform your life. There had to be more in the package than just cash: there had to be something in it for the future and integrity of boxing, there had to be something for my loyal British fans, and there had to be a TV deal which would do more than just put me on the box when I fought.

I knew that the BBC had some money in the bank after missing out with its £123 million bid to continue showing *Match of the Day*, but financially they weren't in the same ballpark as Sky at the start of the negotiations. Sky were the clear front runners for most of the race, despite my preference for terrestrial television. Their offer was extremely attractive and the whole deal was well-structured and fair. They were very reasonable negotiators who respected my concerns and were prepared to be flexible on a number of points. Once it got down to the nitty-gritty, the BBC were not as amenable as Sky on the crucial issue of how much control I would have over my own career and so I swung towards Sky. If everything had been roughly equal in terms of money and my commercial freedom outside of the main boxing deal, the BBC would have won hands down. But that wasn't how it was for several months.

The intervention of Frank Warren complicated matters. He was in Sky's stable, but he knew that I was still interested in the BBC if they tightened up their offer and put a bit more cash on the table. The fact that I was talking to Sky and Warren at the same time led most commentators to believe that I was as good as signed up with both of them. He made me a good offer and I gave it serious consideration. Panos Eliades, Lennox's promoter, also put a lucrative, detailed deal on the table, as did Jonathan Feld and Ben Stone from the World Sports Organisation. The intensity of the negotiations grew by the week, and my lawyers and I had a lot of paperwork to get through and a lot of hard-headed thinking to do. As the year 2000 drew to an end I had offers from two major British television networks, the BBC and Sky, the Warren proposal and five firm offers from top promoters in the States.

When I told Warren that the attraction of terrestrial coverage was pushing me towards the BBC, he said he thought he could swing some kind of deal with both Sky and the BBC. This was chess at its best and Warren was a grandmaster. He was offering me a similar financial package to Sky but wanted almost full control over everything else – in short, a big signing-on fee plus X amount per fight, but he would deal with worldwide rights, sponsorship deals and so on. I've got a lot of respect for Warren and his offer would have made me a very rich man instantly, but I didn't like the idea of not being able to control my own agenda. This was business and I had to do what was right for number one.

Warren talked with the BBC and Sky about me at various points in the negotiations, adding to the uncertainty in the two networks about which one I was going to join. The only two really talking my language were Sky and the BBC. The general line of other contenders in the race was 'You do the fighting, we'll do the thinking', and none of them were prepared to compromise. If they had been, the outcome of those negotiations might have been very different.

I was close to signing the Sky deal, but the BBC kept coming back to me with new offers which got better and better each time I turned my nose up at the last. Slowly, they closed the gap on Sky. As the negotiations reached a climax, there were four runners left in the race: Sky, the BBC, Panos Eliades and Frank Warren. Sky had their noses in front entering the final straight, but the BBC were making a determined late run. Warren and Eliades were still in contention, but they were running out of puff. Around Christmas time, Sky asked me if I would be prepared to do a joint deal with Warren. I said 'No'.

Sky sent over a contract which I was ready to sign, and the details were leaked to one of the Sunday papers. Crucially, Sky hadn't asked for an exclusivity period and on Sunday night the BBC called and said they wanted to make a final offer. I told them it would have to be pretty special if it was to better Sky's. They realised that they were about to lose me, and when we met up on Monday they made me a knockout offer that I couldn't refuse. The BBC were smart enough to insist on a twenty-four-hour exclusivity period which barred me from talking to anyone else. After considering the offer with my lawyers, we decided that we would go with the BBC. They had pulled out all the stops right at the death and, once I had got them close to what Sky were offering, there was never any doubt that terrestrial coverage was going to win the day.

There was always going to be a loser in this race, as well as some very grumpy people who had invested much time and effort. I felt bad in a way because Sky had always been very fair and straight with me, but I couldn't afford to be sentimental. It was business and I had to make the right decisions for my career. I tried ringing Vic Wakeling at Sky to tell him personally that I would not be signing his contract, but he was always in a meeting and in the end I had to break the news to his secretary. She gasped and said, 'Oh, my word!' I like Vic and regard him as an honourable man, and I tried to contact him afterwards to explain my thinking. But Sky took it very badly and word got back to me that they thought I had been using them the whole time in order to get what they thought I had always wanted, a deal with the BBC. But I can say categorically and from the bottom of my heart that that was never the case. Sky led the race from the outset, but they were overtaken at the final hurdle.

The deal was announced in mid-January: an exclusive tenfight, two-year contract for live UK television and radio broadcasting. The BBC also announced they would be screening the World Amateur Championships in Belfast in June – great news for the unpaid sphere of boxing, which had been so starved of exposure since the sport switched to satellite. In the end I had got what I wanted for myself and for my sport. It was a good deal for me, but an even better deal for boxing.

During the negotiations with the television networks I set up my own company, A-Force Promotions, with the help of Hazel, my legal team and the accountants Godfrey Allen. By becoming the director of my own company (with Hazel as company secretary) I had fulfilled another dream that I had been nurturing for years. There was a time when I had been racked with debts, but now I felt really proud and excited as I sat at the head of my own company, ready to take on the world of professional boxing. Sorting out my personal website was also a priority after the company responsible for producing my old one had gone bust a few weeks before Sydney. I quickly struck a deal with secondsout.com, the best boxing site in the world, which allowed my fans to make contact with me again via the web. Slowly everything was falling into place.

My deal with the BBC meant that most of the best-known promoters in Britain were ruled out of my equation. Warren was obviously no go, and Panos Eliades and Barry Hearn's Ringside were out of the picture, because they were all connected to Sky. As a result there were only a few set-ups in the running, and it boiled down to a choice between Jonathan Feld and the World Sports Organisation on one side and Jess Harding and UK Presents on the other. It made sense to go with Jess because of his connections with the BBC – he already had a deal with the BBC to promote *Grandstand* shows and had done a really good job in promoting Spencer Oliver, the European super bantamweight champion.

I think Warren was shocked by my rejection of his offer because not many British boxers turn him down and his offer, in all fairness, was very attractive financially. As far as I'm concerned there's no hard feelings. I just did what was right for Audley Harrison. You win some and you lose some, but either way you just get on with it.

Throughout these protracted and intense negotiations with television networks and promoters, I was also busy trying to find a trainer. The demands of professional boxing are entirely different from those of the amateur code, and in a way I would be starting all over again as a novice in my trade. Getting a trainer of great experience and knowledge whom I could get along with was vital to my future. For a start, I had never boxed for longer than ten minutes at a time, but as a professional you go the distance at half an hour. In amateur boxing you probably throw more punches, but the physical battering

222

you take in the pro ring is far greater and therefore more tiring. I would need to recondition myself physically in order to be able to cope with these new demands, as well as to adapt my technique. Power is much more important in professional boxing, because without helmets and with lighter gloves there is a far greater chance of a knockout or a stoppage. In amateur boxing you rarely see knockouts because of the protective equipment that is worn.

I knew that I would have to explain to people that there was no point trying to run before I could walk. Potentially, a successful career as a professional boxer lies ahead of me, but it's not going to happen overnight. I can't walk off the podium in Sydney and step into the ring with Lennox Lewis or Mike Tyson. In a few years' time, sure, but that time might never come if I get flattened early on, having been over-ambitious in my choice of opponent just to please a demanding press and public. Some people seem to think that the only difference between amateur and professional boxing is that you get paid for one and not the other. That view could not be further from the truth. The only thing they have in common is that both sports take place in a canvas ring.

The only people you meet at the top end of professional boxing have been a success at amateur level, or were so good they were railroaded into the professional arena at an early age, or are still around on the circuit because they are proven, battle-hardened veterans. There are no slouches here. Once a bandwagon is rolling, as mine has been since getting back from Sydney, people's expectations rocket and their patience becomes shorter. They want instant satisfaction and expect instant glory. We live in an age where people will not or cannot wait for success. You only have to look at the cut-throat world of the English football Premier League over the last ten years to understand the increased urgency in people's expectations. If a manager fails to deliver the goods in one or two seasons, more likely than not he will be out on his ear and a new man will be in his place before he has had time to clear the family photographs off his desk.

Personally, I am going to take the slow but sure route by building up my momentum, my confidence and my know-how at the beginning, and then, if all goes to plan, within three or four years I'll be prepared to fight anyone, anywhere, any time. As far as I'm concerned, discretion is the better part of valour and I'm not going to rush into the front line of professional boxing like a have-a-go hero, only to find my career dead in the water.

After returning to England I drew up a shortlist of top trainers who could help me make that transition from amateur to professional boxing. George Benton, who has recently been inducted into the International Hall of Fame, was my number one. He has worked with some of the top boxers including Joe Frazier, Pernell Whitaker, Evander Holyfield and Leon Spinks, and he was said to be very good at training southpaws like me. My second choice was Thell Torrence, another highly respected veteran who had been in the sport for forty years and whose past boxers included Wayne McCullough, Tony Tubbs, Riddick Bowe, Mike McCallum and Ken Norton. Emanuel Steward, Lennox's trainer, was third on my list, but after I met him in Vegas for the Tua fight I struck him off. He just didn't seem like my kind of guy. First impressions count for a lot, and I felt that he wasn't the right man for me at this stage.

My hopes of working with Benton were dashed almost from the outset when Shelley Williams, the woman looking after me in Vegas, told me that he had recently been suffering ill-health and was out of the boxing picture these days. Just in passing I said to her, 'So where does Thell Torrence work out of?' She replied, 'At a gym about a mile up the road from here. We'll go up there if you like.' Five minutes later I was walking into the gym and Thell was walking out with Floyd Mayweather Snr, another top trainer.

'Hi, you must be Thell,' I said and stuck out my hand. We chatted for a minute or so and he obviously thought I was just some guy off the street giving him the jive. But then he clocked who I was and said, 'OK, OK, now I've gotcha. You're the Olympic champion. Nice to meet you.' We chatted for a while about my plans for turning pro and I ended up spending the rest of the day there talking to the other boxers. Crocodile, the guy who walks out in front of Tyson, was in there messing around and all the guys sat me down and started giving me advice. I liked the feel out of the place. It was all very laid back and friendly, and they all said that Thell was the trainer who could help improve my technique.

I returned to my hotel, where a boxer called Foley whom I knew from my Islington days introduced me to Kenny Croom, another well-respected American trainer. Kenny used to work with Thell but they had fallen out over the Ulsterman Wayne McCullough, whom they trained, and hadn't worked with each other for a few years. The pair of them went back ages, and apparently they had been almost like father and son in happier times. I liked Kenny, who impressed me with his knowledge, and he seemed to be interested in working with me. Kenny and Thell, who had worked under the legendary trainer Eddie Futch, were both top trainers, but I wanted to get the low-down on them from someone who had worked with them, so I jumped into a cab and went to see Wayne in his Las Vegas home.

Wayne told me that when the two of them worked together, they were the best. By all accounts, Thell was the wise, old master while Kenny was the hands-on guy, and between them they had had the ability to take a raw boxer and turn him into something special. That's exactly what they had done with Wayne. He had been as raw and wild as they come, but the pair of them turned him into a world champion. Thell told me later that Wayne's improvement under their coaching was one of the proudest achievements of his career. Wayne said he would be amazed if I could get them back together, but if I did I would have the dream coaching team behind me.

The fuse of my determination to make it as a pro had been lit long ago but that trip to Vegas gave me a taste of what it might actually be like. The Lewis v Tua fight took place in the Mandalay Bay Arena on the main Strip, and as I stood under the huge billboard announcing the fight, with the limousines flashing by and the crowd streaming into the auditorium, I felt a great surge of excitement about the possibilities that lay ahead for me. All boxers have to start in places like York Hall in Bethnal Green or the Top Hat in Ealing, with just a couple of hundred people in a smoky crowd, but Vegas is what they are dreaming of. Vegas is the Mecca of boxing, and if you only fight there once you have made it up the long, hard road.

When I got back to England I continued to put my team together. Everything was up for grabs at this stage, but slowly my mind was clearing and I could see the team beginning to take shape. I wanted people I could trust, who I knew would be loyal to me, so I asked my brothers Terry and Rodney to think about leaving their jobs with my Dad and come on board with my training team. I called a friend of mine, Akim, whom I had known for years and had worked with at Islington and Repton, and got him on board in a coaching capacity. Akim, an Algerian by birth, used to box when he was younger but had given it up and was working as a cab driver in east London. I got into the back of his cab one day and we got chatting about boxing and I invited him to come down to Islington. Within a few months he was working there full-time. Now he is helping me out and is hoping to learn more tricks of the trade from Thell and Kenny. At the moment he's very much the apprentice learning the ropes of the professional world, but in three or four years' time I hope to have him working as my house trainer. Charlotte Cowie, the doctor at the Commonwealth and Olympic Games who I got on really well with, has also joined the team and oversees all the medical and physiotherapy matters.

By the New Year Thell and Kenny were the only guys at the races for the training post. I had had fleeting contact with some English trainers but it was the two Americans I wanted on board, partly because they were top-drawer professionals but also because they had a good base and good contacts in the States. I flew back to Las Vegas to find out if they were prepared to work together. Kenny came into the loop first and when Thell came to London to train one of his fighters I worked on him every day. By the time he flew home he said he would give it serious consideration. A few weeks later, Thell called me and said that he and Kenny had met and that they had agreed to work with me. I wanted my early fights to be in Britain, and they were happy to come over to my training camp down at the luxury state-of-the-art Hustyns complex near Bodmin in Cornwall for a month or so before each one, but if I wanted, I could always fly out to Vegas and use their facilities and box with their sparring partners. I was delighted to get the pair of them on board, and now my team was almost complete. All I needed was a manager.

The professional boxing regulations don't allow boxers to be self-managed for their first year, so I had to find someone to fill that role. I considered about a dozen options before approaching Colin McMillan. Colin, or Sweet C as he was known in his boxing days, was just a few years older than me and had recently retired from the ring. He had been one of the best British boxers of his generation and was crowned WBO featherweight champion in 1992 when he beat the Italian Maurizio Stecca. But in the first defence of his title against

Colombian Ruben Palacio later that year he dislocated his shoulder and lost his title, and his career never hit the same heights. But he has remained in boxing ever since and is Secretary of the Professional Boxers' Association. He's a quiet, thoughtful and intelligent character who went back to college (he has seven O levels and three A levels), did a course in journalism and wrote his autobiography, *Fight the Power*. He was someone I could trust, and he was happy with the fact that it was going to be me steering the ship. He was relatively unproven as a manager because he had only just started out, but he had managed his own career at a time when the rules allowed boxers to do so and therefore he knew what he was doing.

I had been hoping for a bit of a rest when I got back from Sydney but, although I wasn't in training because of my knuckle, my feet barely touched the ground for about six months. Every day there were meetings to attend, endless telephone calls to make, piles of documents to be analysed, planes to catch and hotels to check in and out of. It wasn't until I went into training again in March that some peace and order were restored to my life. Each day I was working for about twelve hours, and then in the evening I would head out to some kind of party – a charity event, a film premiere or a celebrity party. The swimmer Sharron Davies, another Olympic gold medallist, described this world as the 'Hello darling, kissy, kissy, Bollinger and bullshit circuit'. To those outside it, it must have seemed that all I was doing was milking my new fame and just enjoying myself when my face was splashed all over the papers and the mags. But I saw it as work because I was raising my profile. A few snipers in the press accused me of caring more about my life as a celebrity than my career as a boxer, but I'm not ashamed to admit that I want to take care of business out of the ring as well as in it. I can see nothing wrong with trying to make the most out of my circumstances. Do the snipers want me to stay in a dark basement until my boxing career is over? I would be a fool if I just ignored the commercial side of my career. There is also an irony in that criticism. If I turned down all media interviews, never turned up to a charity event and effectively shunned the British public, then what? The same critics would accuse me of being sour, ungrateful and selfish.

What is more, I'm the first person to understand that, without my boxing, I wouldn't be a celebrity. I am a celebrity boxer, but if I start failing in the ring much of the celebrity life will disappear too. I don't want to end up on the provincial pantomime circuit playing Widow Twanky. I am a boxer first and a celebrity second. My celebrity is just business pure and simple, and when I take off my gloves I put on my businessman's hat. Before, I had never had a penny in my life, but now I have the chance to improve my circumstances and help out the people around me.

One of the things I did not long after our return from Sydney was attend a reception with the Prime Minister. Britain's Olympic champions were invited to a reception with Tony Blair to celebrate our success. Blair used the opportunity to announce a pledge to offer every pupil the right to two hours of sport a week. It was also announced that the 'New Deal' would be extended to recruit more sports coaches and trainers in a bid to revive competitive sport in school. The package was said to be worth one billion pounds, most of which would go to improving sports facilities and the rest to hiring the 1000 new sports staff. I hope the government carries through its pledge because the quality of school sport is something I have always felt strongly about. It was also rewarding to think that the performance of Team GB had highlighted the value of sport in society, in the joy it brings not just to competitors but also to the wider public. But it was good to hear the Prime Minister showing that he understood how sport also had a beneficial effect in all areas of society in the role it plays in promoting health and general education about life and how it helped reduce youth crime and drugtaking. Sport teaches people to perform under pressure, it teaches you how to work with others in team, and it teaches you how to deal with the joy of victory as well as the despair of defeat. I welcome any pledge to promote sport amongst our youth. Our success at Sydney underlined the importance of funding and investing in the sports infrastructure. The National Lottery helped many of Britain's competitors and medal winners get there in the first place. I'm convinced that without it, Britain's medal tally would have been a mere fraction of what it was.

My image was in big demand when I got back from Sydney. Everyone seemed to want a slice of me, but the skeleton of my past wrongdoings was rattling in the cupboard and I knew I would have to come clean. It was just a matter of time before I woke up one morning to find myself on the front pages. Your past will always catch up with you sooner or later, and I was surprised that no paper had yet picked up on my wild youth and my time in prison. It was hardly a well-kept secret in north-west London. I figured that it was better to volunteer the truth in detail than wait for it to be exposed, with the risk of inaccuracies and exaggerations. I didn't know exactly when I would spill the beans, but after I heard down the grapevine that the *Sunday Mirror* and the *People* were both about to run the story, I got on the phone to the *Sun* and gave them a frank and honest account of what had happened in my youth. The money for the interview went to charity.

I never felt that the revelations were going to damage my reputation. I had somehow developed a squeaky-clean image. I was boxing's Mr Nice Guy, filling the void in the hearts of the British public that was left when Frank Bruno hung up his gloves. According to all the reports I was reading (and thanks to the PR efforts of Clifford and Lindsey at Octagon), the public had the perception that I was friendly, honest, articulate, intelligent and conscientious, and maybe I am all of those things to some degree outside the ring. But there was a danger that I was being built up as the boxing equivalent of Gary Lineker, a kind of Queen Mother with gloves on. There is no better tabloid news story than a supposedly squeaky-clean public figure being exposed as having a dark side or a murky secret.

Another reason why I decided to tell the truth was that I thought it was important for my future sponsors to know everything about the person who was going to be endorsing their product, and I didn't want to deceive anyone and jeopardise a deal. You are chosen by sponsors because they feel that in some way your personality, image and achievements can boost their product, so if the image is tarnished so too is the product you are associated with. I didn't think that being a convicted criminal would necessarily be bad for my image. If anything, it might enhance it and give my profile a harder edge. Boxers are not meant to be nice guys inside the ring. The business of the professional boxer is to batter his opponent, not charm him, to the canvas. Mike Tyson, the baddest of the bad in modern boxing and the biggest box-office draw since Muhammad Ali, was not exactly a country vicar.

By the end of February I had unveiled all the members of my professional team and announced the deal with the BBC. I was all set to embark on the next stage of my career, but there was just one crucial detail missing: my fitness. It had been five months since I had stepped into a boxing ring and I was completely out of condition. The operation on my knuckle had been performed in November in a New York hospital by a leading specialist called Charles Malone, who had also treated Lennox Lewis in his early career. Malone repaired the tendon on my knuckle and fixed my knucklehood before placing it in a cast. The cast had been removed in mid-January, but it wasn't until the end of February that I was given the all-clear to start training.

My weight had steadily crept up during those months of physical inactivity, and getting into shape was the first priority. I had tried to avoid over-indulging, and only once did I go over the top. That was on New Year's Eve in Gran Canaria, where I went with my brothers and some mates and celebrated in style after discovering that I was to receive an MBE. The ceremony at which I would receive my award from the Queen didn't take place until the end of February, when I went along to the Palace with my Dad and my brothers. The Queen is only five foot two, a foot and a half smaller than me, and she had to stand on a platform to pin the medal on my chest. The Queen remembered our conversation from her reception for Team GB and she also made a comment about my new hairstyle. I had taken out the colourful twisted braids from Sydney and sported plaits instead, because I didn't think the twisties were quite right for the occasion. 'What have you done to your hair? It's different,' she said. After the ceremony I was photographed outside Buckingham Palace with my arm around my father, and the next day the picture was plastered all over both the tabloids and the broadsheets. It was a very proud moment for me, but even more so for my Dad. Afterwards we all went to have tea at the Ritz, where they had to lend ties to four of the party so that we would be allowed in. In a way, that day drew a neat line under my Olympic experience and from then on I set about concentrating purely on my boxing future.

In the New Year I read Ian's report into the Olympics and there was not a single word about the Terry Edwards controversy which had dominated every day of the countdown to my first Olympic fight. I find it depressing that the problem has been conveniently swept under the carpet in another case of 'See no evil, hear no evil, speak no evil'. The relationship between the boxers and the management and coaching staff is an important issue that must be addressed if amateur boxing in Britain is to improve at the national level. To ignore problems is not the way forward. But I assume the general line at the ABA has been to dismiss my protests in Sydney with something along the lines of 'It was just Audley kicking up a fuss as usual out in Sydney.'

Before the World Championships in Belfast in June the England boys assembled for a training camp down in Crystal Palace. I called Ian and said I wanted to come down to train with them and give them a pep talk. They were my mates and amateur boxing had been my life for a decade. I thought the presence of an Olympic gold medallist might be an inspiration for them – living, walking, punching proof that British amateurs can be successful. Terry Edwards was there and he said nothing to me. I talked to most of the boxers individually and I was more than a little surprised to hear them tell me that Edwards was apparently going around talking about the great part he played in my success ('If you want to be successful, you have to be like Harrison. Look what we did for him . . .' and so on.) The cheek of it.

Depressingly, the mood among the boys was as low as it had ever been. They were doing the same old routines just as they always had done down the years. It seemed that nothing had been learned and I still believe that if any British boxer does well in Athens 2004 then, like my success, it will be in spite of rather than because of the national coaching set-up. In my view the whole system should be overhauled and fresh blood brought in, Ian should be moved into a supervisory role and allow someone else to take over the hands-on, day-to-day involvement with the boxers, someone like Nicholas Cruz, the Cuban working with Ireland. He knows the international scene as well as anyone and has all the contacts you could want. Unfortunately, I cannot see that happening. Like so many ancient British sporting institutions, the hierarchy is fossilised, the system set in stone and dinosaurs in blazers roam the corridors.

Ironically, England won two medals at the World Championships, with David Haye and Carl Froch (the same Froch who I felt had been badly treated the previous year in Germany) taking silver and bronze respectively. Both performed outstandingly, and if you asked them why they did so well, I believe neither of them would attribute their success to the National set-up. One final illustration of Terry Edwards' negativity was seen (and heard), loud and clear, on British television when Danny Happe from my club, Repton, boxed in his first bout at the championships, which was televised on BBC2. Danny boxed a very strong opponent, who was regarded as the favourite to win the contest. Danny boxed really well and in the last round started opening up to win the contest. Now, for me, I thought that he gave an outstanding performance but as he walked back to the corner, I heard Terry Edwards shout 'Lazy bastard'. His voice was audible through the microphone and obviously Danny was not too happy about it. What the boxers need in the ring is encouragement and a slap on the back when they've done well, not negative words that could lead them to lose confidence in themselves. Danny lost his next fight.

After I had announced my team the rumour mill about my first opponent quickly ground into action, and virtually any bloke over 14 stone was 'named' as my next opponent. Each day during training we would have fun by getting all the papers to see who I was said to be fighting that day. My relationship with the press had changed beyond all recognition by this stage. Before the Olympics I used to give out my mobile phone number to anyone who asked for it, and when a reporter called for an interview I would go and meet him in a pub after training and just have an open chat. It was all very low-key, but unfortunately that kind of approach was no longer feasible. The phones at Octagon never stopped ringing, and if I had said 'Yes' to every request for an interview with papers, magazines, television networks, radio stations and websites, and 'yes' to every request to turn up to one kind of event or other, I would have had no time to sleep or eat, let alone train or have a meeting with a member of my back-up staff or take an evening off. Nowadays, time management and prioritising my commitments have become a vital part of my daily life. But the inevitable consequence was that I would become more remote from the media and speculation would thrive in the void. Some of the stories about me were so far off the mark they could only have been made up.

I read reports quoting rival promoters saying that we were struggling to find an opponent because we were only prepared to pay them peanuts. But these were just cheap shots, and the journalists were naturally happy to go along with them because such things make a good story. If anything, my opponents will do better out of me than out of other boxers. I have always had the interests and rights of boxers at heart and that is why I set up my union in the amateur code. As Secretary of the Professional Boxers' Association Colin, too, is committed to promoting the rights of boxers. We are the last pair of people to trample on the rights and welfare of boxers. But where there is money there is acrimony, and I guess that this is what you have to expect in professional boxing.

In March we announced that my first professional fight would take place at Wembley Arena in May on a night that would be billed as 'The Homecoming'. I had always wanted to make my debut in my own backyard, so that all the people I had grown up with would be there to cheer me on. It wasn't until April, however, that we finally found a suitable opponent, Michael Middleton, a veteran of the circuit with an almost 50–50 record, and who by all accounts would come to fight and not just pick up his cheque, get flattened and go home to Florida. I was clear favourite to win the fight, but everyone we spoke to had said he would give me a decent scrap.

We thought he was the right kind of opponent for my first fight, and I was surprised by the sniping in the press about the quality of his credentials. I am bored with having to say it, because I have said it in virtually every interview I have given since I announced my intention to go professional: I am a novice at the bottom of a steep learning curve. I would need to train intensively and pack in as many fights as possible before I could consider myself a reasonably proficient professional. When a man takes a new job in an office or a factory or a workshop, or as a train driver or a soldier or whatever, he has to learn his trade before he can be expected to excel. Why should the career of a professional boxer be any different?

Most of the journalists were reasonably balanced and fairminded and accepted that Middleton would provide me with the right sort of introduction to pro fighting. There was nothing particularly sophisticated about his style, but this was what I needed: a street fighter who would try and bash me around. In amateur boxing you don't normally get involved in brawls, because the best way to win is by picking off your man with quick hands and quick feet. It's not all about brute power and mixing it with your opponent.

I have always been confident that I would be able to cope with the transition to this new boxing environment. There are two types of fighter in me, and I can switch from one to the other at will. First, there is Audley Harrison the showman. I like to float about the ring toying with my opponent, dazzling with my skills and movement and flashing the odd smile to the crowd. That was the boxer people saw at the Olympics. Then there is the angry Audley Harrison, Mr Nasty. The British public have only seen this side of me twice: first in the 1997 ABA national semifinals when I fought back to win after being knocked down in the opening seconds of the bout. The second occasion was the final of the Commonwealth Games when I was so angry by all the shenanigans going on outside the ring that I stopped my opponent in 63 seconds. When I am in this mode it is not as pretty to watch and I am not as smooth and fluid about the ring, but it is still an awesome spectacle. I can switch into this mode if the bout has turned into a brawl or if my opponent has provoked me in or out of the ring. If someone gives me attitude, I will return it with interest.

Before disappearing from view to my training camp in Cornwall to prepare for the fight, I had lunch with Maureen Bird, my teacher at Harlesden primary school who used to talk to me a lot as a kid. I had not seen her for fifteen years, but after the Olympics she wrote to me and said she was recovering from cancer. It was a very moving letter, saying how my performances at the Games had helped her through her chemotherapy. Over lunch, we talked about my life as a youngster and the other kids she had helped. Some had lost their lives, some were in prison, while others like me had been more fortunate. I remembered her telling me that one day I would make something of myself, and was moved that she had had so much faith in me at a time when other people would have said I was an out-of-control tearaway going nowhere. I was glad that we were able to have lunch together all those years later after I had proved that her faith in me was justified.

Before going to Cornwall, I decided to fly my entire team out for a three-week camp in Lanzarote where I had two main aims: to start working on getting my weight down and to see how the team would gel. I had pulled together a group of individuals who didn't know each other, and it was vital that they all got on well and could work together. The camp proved to be a great success, although my weight wasn't coming off as fast as I had hoped. But by the time we headed down to the

West Country there was still about six weeks for me to get into shape before the fight. Hustyns, my official training camp, is at the bottom of a secluded valley. It is a stunning, peaceful setting tucked away behind electronic iron gates and safe from any prying eyes.

The nearest village is several miles away and the only form of life, apart from the staff who work at the complex, are the thousands of sheep dotted around the neighbouring hills. Hustyns is owned by a Londoner called Terry Johnson, a keen fight fan who has made a fortune in the meat trade. It is in the process of being developed into a luxury retreat with dozens of private chalets built around a central complex with a restaurant, bar, swimming pool, tennis courts, saunas and a gym. At the top of the hill they built, in just seven weeks, a state-of-the-art boxing gym for me with every possible facility I could want, and it was there that I would spend most of our time for the next month. I had met Terry after the Commonwealth Games and we quickly built up a good rapport and he even commissioned his artist friend Mitch to produce a brilliant portrait of me. Terry has followed my career closely ever since – to the point where he and his business associate Steve Crosby took time off from their business commitments to come out and watch my first three fights in Sydney. The Hustyns deal has been good for both of us: I'll promote his complex in return for using his lavish facilities whenever I need to.

Our daily routine started with a run at seven o'clock followed by breakfast; then I would either have a massage or run through some technical routines with Thell and Kenny. All our meals were eaten together around the table in my chalet and were laid on by the chefs at Hustyns. We ate well in Cornwall, nothing fancy but good honest healthy food: steaks, fish, baked potatoes, salads and fruit, but all alcohol was forbidden. After lunch we would relax or attend to business on the phone or e-mail, and then we would tackle the serious business of the day: training and sparring in the gym. We used a number of different sparring partners while we were there, but there were always two in residence: one a powerful heavyweight, the other smaller, lighter and quicker, to help me with the speed of movement and reactions.

Under Thell and Kenny's supervision I made good progress over those few weeks in adapting my technique for the professional ring, learning to slow myself down and pace myself for a longer fight. Also, in pro boxing you have to make your punches both powerful and accurate – you have to open up your opponent and break him down. Fortunately I am quick around the ring for someone of my size, and I can switch my stance to upset my opponent's style and give me more options in opening him up. By the time of the fight I was a lot more confident in my ability to meet the professional challenge. It was unlikely that the fight was going to go the distance, but I had learned enough to handle whatever Middleton could throw at me. As the fight approached, I tied up a deal with my main sponsor, the spread betting company Cantor Index, who have given me a highly lucrative deal over my ten fights with the BBC. In July, Cantor Sport was launched and I was to spearhead the campaign. Cantor boss, Lee Amaitis invited me to the Monaco Grand Prix to celebrate the deal. It was also to give me the opportunity to unwind and take a break from all the tense negotiations.

I planned to fight every six weeks or so to widen my experience, and I wanted the Middleton fight to be the first of five or six fights before the end of the year. Unfortunately, the build-up in the week before the fight was dominated by the rumpus over Middleton's contract. Basically a mistake was made by sending out a contract to him without it going through my lawyers, and there was an error in its terms which Middleton exploited.

Andy Ayling, Warren's right-hand man, got involved with Middleton and, sure enough, the mistake in the documentation was spotted. We held our hands up. From Tuesday night right up to the fight on Saturday we were held to ransom as my lawyers tried to thrash out a compromise deal. Middleton was in for a windfall he would never have got if everything had been done properly from the outset but, egged on by others, he saw a chance to increase his purse. And, to be fair, several other boxers would have tried to do the same. I knew that negotiations were still taking place on Saturday, but I thought everything had been sorted out by the time we arrived at the arena from the Wembley Plaza Hotel next door, where we had been staying for the week before the fight. Even when the start of the fight was delayed I had no idea, while I was getting ready in the changing room, that the contract was the cause of it. I thought there was a technical hitch, or that the undercard fights had run over time. It was only afterwards that I discovered the wrangling had gone right to the wire and that Middleton was refusing to fight until the matter was resolved.

I didn't feel angry about what happened because we were all new to the professional game and inevitably we were going to make a few mistakes until we found our feet. I would rather do so at that stage than later. We did some things well, and some less well. Predictably, my 'friends' in the rival camps were only too keen to kick up a stink and blacken my name and that of all those associated with me. Unfortunately, everyone assumed it was Colin's fault as he was my manager, and he was the one who had to go to Middleton to try and sort it out when the mistake was revealed. Some bad things were said about Colin and his integrity was called into question, particularly because he was Secretary of the PBA and had always been a champion of boxers' rights. But it wasn't his fault and anyone who questions the integrity of the man is way off the mark and is just trying to score cheap points. Colin McMillan is an honourable man.

I was completely unaware of all this squabbling behind the scenes, so I wasn't distracted by it as I walked out into the arena at Wembley. I loved the whole night. The fight was taking place just a few streets from my stomping ground as a child, and it felt exactly like that as I strode down the steps amid a deafening roar from my fans, with the TV pictures being beamed to twenty countries. There were hundreds of my friends in a crowd of 5500 as well as a load of celebrities including Lennox, Linford Christie, Darren Gough, Pauline Quirke, Tim Foster, David Dein and his lovely wife, Tamsin Outhwaite, Nick Hancock and Gary Lineker.

The atmosphere was unbelievable, and when the chant 'Audley, Audley' went up I felt like I was back in Sydney. As I stood backstage waiting to make my entrance down the long stairs, Middleton slipped in at the side door, wearing a black gown with the hood up. Word had obviously got around about the contract problems, and as he shuffled up to the stage the crowd gave him a sound booing. I thought his choice of music, 'Money for Nothing' by Dire Straits, was terrible, but I guess it was meant to be an ironic joke. Boom, boom. I towered over the man and he must have seen from the look in my eyes that there was only one place he was going that night – to the canvas.

I was expecting a brawl from him, but after I had hit him with a couple of jabs he was already reeling. I wanted the fight to go at least a couple of rounds, so I could put on a bit of a show for the fans, but it wasn't to be. He was bloody and bowed with just 165 seconds on the clock, and the fight was over. I knew I would beat the guy, but we had been told he could scrap a bit and would keep coming at me even if I knocked his head into next week. And to be fair to him, he didn't want the fight to end. I felt a huge sense of anti-climax when it was stopped – I had been enjoying myself, and part of the point of these early fights was to get as much competitive experience as possible. But my first fight in my own backyard was always going to be a homecoming party first and a fight to remember second. The fact is that within a year most people would have forgotten about Middleton and I would hope to have moved on to bigger and better things. The plan was to move up a level with each fight, and within six months to a year we would know whether I was ready to start challenging for titles.

There is a romance about the Olympics which creates a universal sense of goodwill. Everyone is on your side; everyone is your mate. We are all pulling for Britain and the romantic ideal of the Olympics. So long as you do your best, everyone will give you a slap on the back. But the world of professional boxing is an entirely different kettle of fish – a shark-infested world where people will tear you to bits if they have a chance. All I have to do is win my fights and prove to them that their scepticism was wrong. I have learned from my time on the streets that revenge is often best eaten cold. There is no point steaming into a bunch of people taking liberties when there is nothing to gain from it. It is better to make a tactical withdrawal and then prove yourself to them when the time is right.

Popularity is a fickle, often short-lived thing, but while I have got it I'm going to enjoy it and at the moment I'm having fun. I'm enjoying my life. The whole fame experience will never go to my head because I know it can turn a man into an arrogant, spoiled brat without realising it. Without mentioning any names, you could fill several boxing rings with the guys who have thought they were the business and then – literally – ended up flat on their faces. The margins of error in boxing are very fine and one moment's attention can leave you and your career lying face down on the canvas with your popularity and influence streaming towards the exit signs. Right now, at the start of my pro career, I can say with total honesty that my success in Sydney has not changed me as a character, even a little. Ask anyone close to me and they will tell you that Audley is the same as he was when he was walking the streets of north-west London (just causing a bit less trouble).

I have stated publicly that I want to be heavyweight champion of the world and a handful of critics – some in rival boxing camps and some journalists connected with those camps – have been quick to mock me for saying that. They say I have created a rod for my own back, that I have done nothing in boxing yet and that I should keep my mouth shut. They are entitled to their opinions.

What they have to understand is that it is not right for me to be sceptical about myself. What kind of ambition is it that does not set its sights on the highest pinnacle? Aim for the sun and you may reach it, but failing that, you may hit the moon. Aim for the moon and you are unlikely ever to get off the launching pad. My point is that it makes no sense for me to say that I intend to be European champion in five years, because with my ambitions set that low I'll get into the mind-set where I think that achieving that goal is good enough. I have to believe that I can go the whole way. There is no alternative. Boxing is partly about natural talent and technical ability, partly about the team you put together and partly about preparation, but unless I go into the ring thinking that I have what it takes as a character to become the world champion then I might as well stay in the locker room. More than anything else, boxing is about self-belief. To limit your ambition is to undermine that self-belief. Without dreams, there is no hope.

In five years' time I'm either going to be heavyweight champion of the world or I'm not. I believe I've got the talent to achieve that. All I need is the right training and conditioning and the right choice of opponents along the way. What is more, I cannot see anyone else on the heavyweight horizon who you could honestly say is head and shoulders above the rest. Holyfield and Tyson are out of the picture, and by the time I am in a position to start challenging at that level Lennox Lewis will be in his late thirties and will probably have retired. But if I don't realise that dream I'm not going to start crying. I will have tried my best, and if my best is not good enough then so be it. But what I will say is that no one gave me the slightest chance of winning Olympic gold, but I came through a very strong field to win in style. Write me off at your peril.

I have a number of ambitions outside of boxing. I believe that I am a good businessman, and after retiring I might go the Richard Branson route and try and build up the A-force brand in other areas. I want to get into the movie business and I would also like to have my own talkshow, make a record, fly a plane, climb a mountain: in short, I want to keep challenging myself and search for new adventures, reach new heights and fathom uncharted territories. Live your life and learn to love adversity and you will learn to love life. Live the life you love and love the life you lead, if you're positive you will surely succeed.

But no matter what happens I will always have my Olympic gold medal, and my sense of pride from winning that will never be diminished by anything that lies ahead. Terry Spinks and Dick McTaggert were cheered to the rafters for decades after their Olympic victories in Melbourne in 1956, and their achievements came at a time when no one was surprised because British amateur boxing was thriving. My Olympic triumph was Britain's first in thirty-two years. No one will ever be able to take that achievement away from me. I had spent nearly two years in custody when I took up boxing. My life appeared to be going nowhere, but I rebuilt it bit by bit. Everything I did was the result of my own determination and initiative. I shunned a life of crime, I struggled with huge debts to give myself an education, and I battled against every setback to become the most successful amateur British boxer for two generations. Not bad for a lazy bugger.